Understanding Your Baby

A WEEK-BY-WEEK DEVELOPMENT &
ACTIVITY GUIDE FOR PLAYING
WITH YOUR BABY FROM BIRTH TO
12 MONTHS

AYELET MARINOVICH

Strength In Words LLC
Mountain View, California

ISBN: 978-1-7321329-0-0

eISBN: 978-1-7321329-1-7

Contents

Introduction

Regardless of who you are, where you come from, what language or languages you speak, you and I (and anyone who considers themselves a parent or caregiver) are each ultimately responsible for raising humans. When we understand more about how humans all over the world develop and learn, we feel more empowered to parent.

Regardless of whether you're a first time or a "seasoned" parent or caregiver, when you have an infant, you are in the thick of it. Becoming a parent (or any type of caregiver – I'll use these words interchangeably throughout) to a new person is an enormous undertaking. Regardless of how much (or how little) we think we know about babies, there is so much to learn. I want you to remember that we *all* feel vulnerable, and we *all* want the best for the children in our care.

This book does not aim to cover the divisive topics on which we tend to stand vehemently behind opposing lines. This is about our babies. This is about you. I want to provide gentle support to help you understand and connect with your baby, so you can move *together* through the first year of caregiving. We mix the developmental research (the science) with the creative ways to support the developmental stages your baby moves through (the art).

We are going to get to the heart of what it is to be a caregiver of infants.

Infants (and toddlers) learn through observation, imitation, and interaction. When we learn more about what "play" looks like using very simple materials, we feel some peace of mind that we all crave as parents. Peace of mind is what we all want: we want to know that we are doing all we can to raise decent human beings.

That's what I aim to provide at **Strength In Words**. That's the kind of community that I'm fostering, and that's what I'd like to begin to offer you with this book. It's all about finding the joy in the mayhem. Parenting infants and toddlers is crazy – I'm not going to tell you I can take that away... I can't! What I can do is to help you find the joy in the connection, and start to build the foundation for a lifetime of learning.

My Journey Into Parenthood

I was 10 weeks pregnant with my first baby when my husband and I moved across the world. Surrounded by new people, customs, systems, and struck by the newness of the journey toward parenthood, I was very focused on creating connections.

When my baby was born, I decided to combine my professional background and my desire to create a safe, social learning space for myself and my baby along with other caregiver-baby pairs. I started to devise a curriculum that was based on my own developmental knowledge, that of my friends and colleagues in early learning, a ton of developmental research, and information and experiences I integrated as a mother along the way.

Through this process, I learned several things. First, I learned to become more confident as a mother. I learned to listen to myself, to my baby, and to other caregivers, distilling information that was pertinent to me (and to my baby) and of interest to the other caregivers around me. Perhaps most importantly, I learned just how powerful knowledge can be.

There are so many divisive topics in the world of parenthood. In the beginning, I was very fixated on these issues, because the choices we make about how to nourish and support our babies feel all-encompassing in those early days of parenthood. These are individualized, personal choices. I searched for information – and often, I was met with "experts" and "solutions," when really, what I needed was knowledge. When I stepped back and remembered how much I understood about how babies learn, I began to feel more connected to my baby – and more empowered as a mother to make decisions about all aspects of parenthood. When I shared that information with other caregivers, they felt the same way. Now, I'd like to share it with you.

I also want to encourage you to reach out and find your communities of support. Whether you have friends and family with other small babies, you take advantage of local playgroups, classes, or library story times, it's the support of other families that keeps us afloat during a year that can have both beautiful highs and dark, dark lows. The opportunity to observe other caregiver-baby pairs and to speak openly and frankly with other parents who are on the same journey offers us a chance to gain some perspective (during a time when it can be very difficult to see past that which is directly in front of us), and to synthesize information.

One of the wonderful benefits of the Strength In Words Community LAB is that we have created a platform for both parent support and parent education that can be accessed in the comfort of your own home. Our community hub allows you to connect with other parents and caregivers (all around the world!) on the same journey, asking the same questions, and sharing experiences and ideas – in a facilitated, respectful setting that values education and ideas, rather than one-size-fits-all "advice." We meet for live virtual events (parent support groups, developmental music classes, and Q&A Workshops with professionals and special guests addressing various areas of early development and family health), we house an ever growing, well-organized resource library, and we are a social network created to help each member feel nurtured – so you can nurture your tiny human. If you're interested in learning more about the Strength In Words Community LAB, you can find us online at community.strengthinwords.com.

My Professional Background

I want to start by saying that I certainly don't know everything there is to know about infant development. That said, over the last several years, I've sharpened and deepened my professional knowledge as a practicing pediatric speech-language pathologist. I've mothered my way through two very different early parenting experiences. I've also interviewed countless professionals about the ways we can support infants and toddlers in the areas of cognition, communication, motor/sensory, and social/emotional development, and read a good deal of the developmental research and literature that informs how (and what) we practice as professionals in the world of early child development.

Much of my professional background is in early intervention. I have dedicated my career to working with "early communicators," primarily with infants and toddlers and their adult counterparts. In the world of education, the term "early learning" often refers to children who are not yet school-aged, but who are in the pre-school years... but we know that babies are learning from day one (and even before). We know that their parents and caregivers are learning, too.

Those first few years of life set the stage for the rest of our child's life. Now, I don't say that to add to the incredible pressure we have as parents and caregivers to "do enough" for our children. That weight is already more than sufficiently heavy! In my mind, it's about simplification. We desperately need to simplify our lives. We need access to quality over quantity. Our children need high quality interactions and opportunities to engage with the world, *not* "the latest learning toy." We, their caregivers, need access to high quality information and high quality interactions, and an opportunity to reflect upon what's working and what's not working – *not* a million mommy blogs and fancy craft ideas on Pinterest.

When we (as parents and caregivers) feel confident that we have access to resources that actually make a difference, we feel empowered to do the job of raising tiny humans. As an early interventionist, I strive to work within family-centered practice. This means that I help families maximize the opportunities for play and development within naturally occurring, everyday activities, and using materials that already exist within the home. Instead of being the therapist who walks into a family's home with a "magical" bag of therapy materials, I see my job as that of a facilitator or coach, helping families see the power of routines-based intervention, and focusing on "routines" that are most important to that family. A routine is any activity that is regularly occurring, that has fairly predictable steps, and that has a clear beginning and end. We all engage in different kinds of routines in our homes – caregiving routines (e.g., eating, dressing, washing), play routines (e.g., infant massage, dance parties, book-reading), social routines (e.g., performing a finger play, playing peek-a-boo, tickling), and daily tasks (e.g., getting the mail, putting on shoes before we go outside). When we can identify these and maximize their value, we can make a huge difference within simple activities (that we're already doing)!

At Strength In Words, we create resources to improve the quality of your family's interactions by sharing easily digestible information that increases your knowledge about early development. Come join our community of families and help us spread the word about Strength In Words.

Thanks for making me part of your journey through parenthood,

Ayelet Marinovich, M.A., CCC-SLP

https://www.strengthinwords.com

© 2018 Strength In Words LLC

How To Use This Book

There's no such thing as a step-by-step parenting guide. No two families – and no two children – are the same. This book is *not* a "how-to" guide to the first year of parenting. There's no way (at least, for me) to write a book like that, because I don't much care for "one-sized-fits-all" approaches to parenting. There *are*, however, universal truths about how humans develop. I've broken these down into 52 little pearls of wisdom, anchored in developmental research and helping you to utilize what you already have: your body, your voice, and a few simple objects (already) in your environment that can be used to help you maximize your interactions with your baby.

The content of this book can be considered an infant guide and "curriculum" for parents and caregivers of babies from 0 – 12 months, delivered in a manner that can be easily consumed by new (exhausted) parents. In this book, you'll find 52 easily digestible "modules" on which you can focus – one for each week of your baby's first year of life. You can download the handy **"Understanding Your Baby: Week-By-Week Calendar"** that comes with your purchase of this book (find that and all the other bonus materials here: https://www.strengthinwords.com/book-bonus), print it out and stick it up on your refrigerator or on a wall of your nursery so you'll get in the habit of referring back to this book when you need a gentle guide.

Each of these modules includes concise "nuggets" of developmental information, paired with simple, practical ideas that require little to no materials. Each one addresses major areas of development, including: cognitive, communicative, motor, and social/emotional development. You can think of this as a weekly "check-in," not simply a list of developmental milestones! This curriculum is based on developmental research and universal guidelines for early learning, and is useful for *all* families – those whose infants are moving along a typical progression of development, and those experiencing (or at risk for) developmental delays.

Paired with your membership to the Strength In Words Community LAB (our virtual parent support and parent education hub), you'll have the resources you need to feel more confident in your parenting, and to feel more connected to your baby, to yourself in your new identity as a caregiver, and to a positive community of support that you can access from the comfort of your own home. You can take a free 1-week trial of the Community LAB by joining us here: https://community.strengthinwords.com

IN CASE YOU'VE SKIPPED DOWN TO THESE "HOW TO" STEPS, HERE'S WHAT YOU NEED TO KNOW:

1. Head over to https://www.strengthinwords.com/book-bonus and download your free bonus materials, including your week-by-week calendar. I don't know about you, but placing a reminder right in front of me is the only way I'll be more likely to use tools and resources in which I've invested. And I want you to use this book!
2. You can jump into the book at any stage. If you are still

expecting or have a newborn, start from chapter one, week one. If your baby is already 3 months old, go ahead and skip to chapter two (and so on)!

3. Throughout the book, I may refer you to additional resources on the Strength In Words website. The aforementioned link will also help guide you to those resources, where they're listed and broken down by chapter.

That's it! I'll be here for you every step of the way – don't hesitate to reach out on social media! I always love to hear from readers. If you've been inspired by something you've learned or tried, go ahead and use the hashtag #strengthinwords – join other families and let us know what *your* family life looks like!

Instagram: @strengthinwordspics

Facebook: @strengthinwords and @understandingyourbaby

Twitter: @ayeletmarino

On Early Development and Play

You Already Have All The Materials You Need: The Benefits of Open-Ended Play

We are already engaging in the kinds of activities that can make a huge impact on our baby's development (caregiving routines, short play routines, and other daily routines). We also already have the materials we need. We all have open-ended play materials lying around our homes, often in plain view. Open-ended materials are simply items that can be used in lots of different ways and in different environments (say, indoors or outdoors), and can be combined and often redesigned or repurposed by a young child in any way that child or her playmates decide.

These materials often allow children to explore and be inventive in the way they are used... babies are naturally inventive, and (depending on your little one's age) you might have already noticed that your baby is often more interested in the regular objects you have lying around the house rather than the fancy toy that the grandparents purchased for the holidays....

Often, young children end up exploring their environment, taking regular objects, and converting them into toys – a prime example of this is the infant who is on the move, sitting up, and able to open the kitchen cabinets to take out her favorite "drum set," a pot and a pan! An older toddler who is engaging in what's called "symbolic play," or the kind of play that uses objects to symbolize and imitate what they've seen others doing, might take out the same pot and pan, and a wooden spoon, and start to stir, imitating her parents in the kitchen.

So, open-ended materials often encourage creative thinking in that a child must explore its properties and how it might be used.[1] In addition, when you have a house or play area full of open-ended materials, they can often be used together in new and inventive ways. A scarf or blanket might serve as a great hiding place for a building block or even a Tupperware container (which can then "peek-a-boo!"). A cork might balance beautifully on top of a wooden block or a toothbrush holder, or fit inside a paper towel roll. A coaster might fit inside one cup, but not another.

Open-ended materials often encourage problem-solving.[2] *What fits where? How can I get this to work that way? Can I get that out if I pull this?* Using open-ended materials also tends to save us a lot of money. Not only do we often save money by using common household objects or natural materials instead of expensive electronic gadgets that purport themselves to "teach such and such" skill, our children are going to learn best through exploring, interacting, and imitating us!

Open-ended toys are really just materials that your little one

1. Torelli, L. (1992). The developmentally designed group care setting: A supportive environment for infants, toddlers, and caregivers. In E. Fenichel (Ed.), Zero to Three child care classics: 7 articles on infant/toddler development (pp. 37–40). Arlington, VA: Zero to Three/National Center for Clinical Infant Programs.
2. Daly, L., & Beloglovsky, M. (2015) Loose parts: Inspiring play in young children. St. Paul, MN: Redleaf Press.

can explore, without a set agenda. And when we encourage our tiny people to become more creative, that will serve them well down the road: we encourage them to be active participants in their lives.

What We Need To Understand About Play With Infants: It Looks Different

Adults often think of play in adult notions. We might think of "playing a game," which has rules, follows an often linear trajectory, and depends on others doing things "correctly" to be played. Babies play, too, but it can be difficult to see and to understand what it is they're doing – or how we can play with them – because it requires a shift in our own mentality. Play for infants (and toddlers) is not terribly linear! When an infant sees a block, she doesn't automatically think, "this is for stacking and building." That is something that she will learn over time (and often, she will learn that knocking them down is incredibly fun *before* she discovers the joy in building). When an infant sees a book, he doesn't automatically think, "let's read this from cover to cover." There are layers of skills that emerge over time, through various experiences with those play materials, that lay the foundation for skills such as constructing and reading.

What comes first is observation, exploration, imitation, and interaction. This is why you'll often hear educators who work with infants and toddlers suggest that you "follow your child's lead." If your baby is mouthing a book, block, coaster, or rattle, chances are, she's learning about it. If she's banging a maraca against the floor instead of shaking it in the air, she may be experimenting with its properties: how heavy it is, how much force her body requires to push into the floor, which direction her arm can move, how loud something is (and whether it will be so loud the next time around). Young children are constantly experimenting with the world around them – it's how they play, and it's how they learn.

We can model the way we play with an object, giving our baby the chance to observe and imitate. When he's ready, assuming his body is able to, he will imitate our actions. We can narrate what we're doing, what our child is doing, provide musical experiences, early literacy experiences, and movement and sensory experiences for our babies. In so doing, we provide our children with the tools to learn, and with an environment that encourages social/emotional development, cognitive development, communication development, and motor development.

Holistic Learning

Infants and toddlers learn "holistically," meaning that although there are various areas of learning and development, they are all very much connected in the first three years of life.

Throughout this period, a child may focus on a certain type of skill or interest in one domain, but process all kinds of information simultaneously.[3] For a further discussion of this topic, please listen to the Strength In Words podcast episode, **"Holistic Learning."**

The bonding that can form from simply being with your baby allows you as the caregiver to start to watch and read your little one's interests, preferences, and behaviors even from the first few months. We tend to start paying attention to things like motor abilities and language development later on because it starts to become very obvious when a child is suddenly able to

3. California Department of Education, California Infant/Toddler Curriculum Framework, Sacramento, 2012, pg. 133.

roll over or crawl, or when she starts to wave or say her first word.

We have to remember that these capabilities don't just magically appear the day we witness them – they're the result of layers of learning, practicing, and problem solving. That pointing gesture that is so communicative came from months of your baby experimenting with the way her arm moves up and down (gross motor), practice with isolating a finger (fine motor), attending to the ways you talk to her (cognitive), becoming aware of those around her (social/emotional), and also imitating and understanding that lifting one's finger and pointing in the direction of a person or object can be symbolic of a request or an attempt to draw the attention of another person (communicative).

The point is, we have to learn to give our young children opportunities to experiment and learn, and we need to give our babies the benefit of the doubt that they are learning all the time.

Questions and Concerns About Development

The information and activities we will discuss in this book are largely applicable to both typically developing infants, as well as those with developmental delays and special needs. The ideas presented in this book are for informational purposes only and are not medical advice. This book is not meant to replace an individualized treatment plan developed as the result of in-person assessment, clinical observation, and collaboration between therapist and caregiver.

If you are concerned about your child's development or functional abilities, please seek information from your child's pediatrician, or seek out the services of a developmental pediatrician or local pediatric therapist within a specialty area (i.e., physical therapist, speech-language pathologist, occupational therapist, etc).

Although I am a registered and licensed speech-language pathologist, this curriculum is *not* a place for therapeutic recommendations or interventions to address specific delays or diagnoses. The ideas presented here are intended to be used for play in a *supervised* setting. If you have questions or concerns about presenting any activity to your infant, speak with your baby's medical professional beforehand.

Always ensure that you are present and attentive when presenting an activity to your baby. Strength In Words LLC is not liable for any injury incurred while replicating an activity found within this book.

CHAPTER 1

Within this chapter, I'll suggest additional resources for you to explore on the Strength In Words website. You can find all of those resources organized by chapter here: https://www.strengthinwords.com/book-bonus

1 WEEK OLD: SENSES AND MOODS

Senses and Moods (Social / Emotional Development)

Brand new babies are learning to take an interest in senses – what they see, hear, feel, smell, and how they move. They are also learning to calm themselves... through you![1]

From the first weeks of life, babies respond to care differently – some are more sensitive to their environment than others. [2] Some can more easily understand the messages their senses take in.

1. National Research Council and Institute of Medicine, From Neurons to Neighborhoods: The Science of Early Childhood Development (Washington, DC: National Academies Press, 2000).
2. Graven, S.N., Browne, J.V. (2008). Sensory Development in the Fetus, Neonate, and Infant: Introduction and Overview. Newborn and Infant Nursing Reviews, 8(4), 169-172.

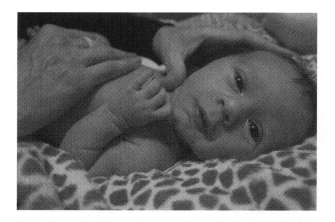

WHAT YOU CAN DO

Watch and attend to your baby's different moods

- **When she is calm and alert, lay down next to her and watch her**

  - Speak to her softly about what she sees, hears, smells, feels with her fingers, what her body is doing

- **When she cries, offer comfort through:**

  - You (your touch, smell, voice, movement, milk)

  - Through an object that may have your smell

  - With a change in "sensory" environment (dimmer lights, less noise, varied temperature, different materials around her)

2 WEEKS OLD: HOLD ME CLOSE

Hold Me Close (Motor Development)

Your baby is most likely happiest when he is in your arms.

He can smell you, touch you, feel your breath... all his sensory needs are met.

Not only are you providing him with a sense of security and with time together, you are also helping your baby with his motor development, *while* you are holding him! [3]

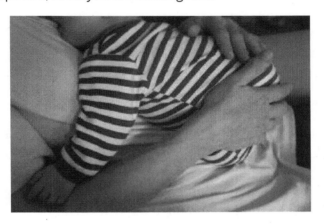

WHAT YOU CAN DO

Hold your baby in different positions, or on alternate sides of your body (while continuing to support his head).

- **This gives him different perspectives**

  - It also strengthens various muscle groups

- **Bring him to different places**

  - Outside, to various rooms, to the window

  - Give him a variety of views and sensations, such as natural light from the window, fresh air on his face, the sound of birds or of wind...

3. California Department of Education, California Infant/Toddler Curriculum Framework, Sacramento, 2012, pg. 133.

- *Great Resource:*

  ◦ Check out the Strength In Words podcast episode, **"Secret Guide to Tummy Time,"** featuring occupational therapist and blogger, Rachel Coley of the blog, *CanDo Kiddo,* and our ideas for **high contrast images to support movement**

3 WEEKS OLD: SOUND AND SOURCE

Sound and Source (Communicative Development)

Even in utero, research confirms that babies recognize the sound of their mothers' voices.[4] Once born, they learn to associate comfort with the voices they hear most often.

Though other senses may not be as developed in the early days, your baby should be able to hear quite well (assuming the ear and auditory system are intact and healthy)... though she cannot yet locate the source of a sound.

4. DeCasper, A., & Fifer, W. (1980). Of human bonding: Newborns prefer their mothers' voices. Science, 208, 1174-1176.

WHAT YOU CAN DO

Speak and make noises to your baby – it doesn't matter what you talk about! Your baby is listening to the sounds, melody and rhythm of your speech... and, over time, she will learn to understand the content of your words.

- **Help your baby to make the connection to the source of a sound you make, and vary the types of sounds**

  ◦ Lay with your baby on one side or the other, sit/stand closer or farther away when you speak to her

  ◦ Vary your volume at times, by speaking or singing more loudly and more softly (remember, your baby may startle at sounds that are too loud or sudden)

  ◦ Make or play music (recorded and/or your live singing voice), or play an instrument – whether it's a violin or a rattle!

4 WEEKS OLD: STAY IN TUNE WITH BABY

Stay In Tune With Baby (Cognitive Development)

Even very young infants demonstrate preferences, as seen through their facial expressions, gaze, sounds, and movements.

When you pay close attention to your baby's actions, you show him that you are trying to be attuned to his needs! [5]

---

5. Bergen, D., Reid, R., and Torelli, L. (2009). *Educating and Caring for Very Young Children: The Infant/Toddler Curriculum* (2nd ed.). New York, NY: Teachers College Press.

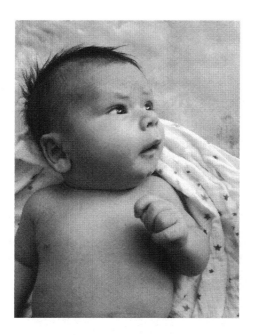

WHAT YOU CAN DO

When you respect your child's initiative, you demonstrate to him that his behavior has an effect on you and on his environment. This is a wonderful example of how, over time, your baby will learn about cause and effect.

- **If your baby cries, turns away, or grimaces to show he is upset or finished with an activity, change the activity and/or the environment**

  ◦ If this is impossible to do in the immediate term, talk to him and tell him why, and that you hear his desire to do something else

- **If your baby wiggles his arms and/or legs, watches intently, or vocalizes "happily," keep doing what you're doing!**

- Stay focused on him for a few minutes longer, and try not to be disrupted by technology or other outside forces!

5 WEEKS OLD: SOCIAL SMILE

Social Smile (Communicative Development)

Typically, babies develop what is known as a "social smile," or an intentional smile, somewhere between 6-8 weeks.

In the early days and weeks after birth, you may see your baby turn her mouth upwards, seemingly smiling... though this is beautiful to witness, it is most likely your baby passing gas!

A social smile indicates that your baby is beginning to make connections about human behavior. [6]She realizes that returning your smile keeps your attention. This is a wonderful early step in back-and-forth communication, and in developing her self-esteem, as it lets your baby know that you think her feelings are important.

Remember that the more you smile at your baby, the more your baby will watch and try to imitate (just as she watches and listens when you speak, read aloud, or sing to her).

6. Wormann, V., Holodynski, M., Kartner, J., Keller, H. (2013). The Emergence of Social Smiling: The Interplay of Maternal and Infant Imitation During the First Three Months in Cross-Cultural Comparison. Journal of Cross-Cultural Psychology, 45(3), 339-361.

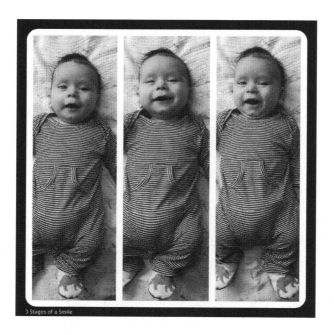

3 Stages of a Smile

WHAT YOU CAN DO

When your baby is relaxed and alert, bring her close and smile widely, speaking to her gently

- **At this age, your baby sees best only up to 12 inches away**

  - This is about the space between your face and where you hold her to your body in your arms)

  - Make sure you are close enough to be seen

- **If you don't know what to say...**

  - Simply greet your baby, playing with your voice's tones (going up and down, speaking in a slightly sing-song pitch).

  - Vary the speed at which you speak or sing to your baby,

going from fast to slow or slow to fast, so she listens to the changes in your voice

- ◦ Go from farther away to closer to her, burying your head in her tummy – she may find this close contact and vocal play to be hilarious.=

- **You don't need to wait until 6-8 weeks to play in this way**

  - ◦ Though you need not expect a wide grin in response prior to this, your baby will take in your actions and start to make the important connections that she can affect her environment and the people in her life

6 WEEKS OLD: BABY TAKES A BREAK

Baby Takes A Break (Social/Emotional Development)

Though very young babies benefit from interaction, movement, visual input (things they see) and auditory input (sounds, or things they hear), they also have a hard time processing these things when too much input is presented at once or for too long.

Young babies don't have a very long attention span, and can be quickly overwhelmed by sensory information they take in (through their eyes, ears, through touch, etc). They often play (make eye contact, touch toys, etc.) for brief periods of time before they may become "over-stimulated." Research indicates that cue-based care for infants (the provision of physical care such as holding, touching, or feeding when responding to their needs) is associated with more settled babies. [7]

7. St James-Roberts I., Alvarez M., Csipke E., Abramsky T., Goodwin J., Sorgenfrei E. Infant crying and sleeping in London, Copenhagen and when parents adopt a "proximal" form of care. Pediatrics 2006; 117:e1146-55.

WHAT YOU CAN DO

Your baby will let you know when he is done playing, but it is up to you to read his cues. It may be that he cries or fusses, rubs his eyes, turns his head, arches his back, or falls asleep.

- **Watch what she "tells" you, and respect this early communication by giving him a rest (changing or pausing the activity)**

  - His body may change – in color (pale or bright red), breath (fast or choppy breathing), or movement (jerky or shaky), or his behavior may change [8] – going from alert and engaged to:

8. The NICU Experience: Its Impact and Implications; Virginia Early Intervention Conference; Roanoke, VA; March 7-8, 2005. Presenter: Barbara Purvis, M.Ed., NTAC Technical Assistance Specialist.

- He may "space out" – he may suddenly look away and stare at "nothing"

- He may "shut down" – he may go from engaged to suddenly quite sleepy

- He may "switch off" – he may continually turn away from you if you keep trying to engage

- **You might offer comfort through:**

  ○ You (your touch, smell, soft voice, milk) – the *suckling reflex* may calm him

  ○ Decreased stimulation – speak more quietly, remove some of the objects around him

  ○ A change in "sensory" environment (dimmer light, less noise, colder or warmer temperature, different materials around him

7 WEEKS OLD: ROOM TO MOVE

Room to Move (Motor Development)

Babies spend the early days, weeks and months learning to move... being confined in equipment does not allow them to do this! [9]

Other than in your arms, the safest position, and most beneficial for learning about her body, is laying down on a flat, firm surface. Laying in a car seat or even in a "Moses basket" or bassinet for much or all of the day doesn't give her access to much physical input from the environment.

9. Pica, R. (2010, July). Babies on the Move. Young Children, pp. 48-49.

WHAT YOU CAN DO

Engineer and change the environment!

- **Place her on her back on a clean, firm surface (a blanket on the floor is really all you need!), allowing her to stretch or wave her arms and legs.**

  - You might put tissue paper (or any crinkled paper) near her hands or feet, so that her movements result in making a sound

- **Place her near a shatterproof mirror where she can see herself – she may be fascinated by watching her own movements!**

  - Find a sheltered place outside (ensuring she is warm or cool enough) and give her opportunities to spend time connecting with the fresh air, in the grass or in the snow!

- **Start giving your baby opportunities for "tummy time" from as early on as you can**

- For typically-developing babies, this can be very shortly after they're born! *If you haven't been doing this regularly, it's not "too late" to start!*

  - Lay down next to her and gently speak to her, then go to the other side (or have your partner on the other side). Take turns speaking her name.

  - Sing a song, say a nursery rhyme, or tell her a story – while you're down on her level.

  - If you ever feel you are "bombarding" her with sound and stimulation, call her name once and wait before you speak again... it will likely take her several seconds to respond, but if you give her time to process the sound of your voice, she may respond a few seconds later. If she does not, try again, or limit your input.

8 WEEKS OLD: LISTEN TO MUSIC

Listen to Music (Cognitive Development)

Exposing your baby to music is a very natural way to provide the opportunity to hear different kinds of patterns. [10]

Different types of tonalities help express different "character" in music – whether it sounds joyful, dark, excited, etc. Rhythms express the arrangement of songs, and give the beat and stress we hear.

Most children's music in Western culture is in a "major" tonality (usually sounding happy and upbeat) and has a "duple meter" (referring to the rhythm having a count of 1-2, 1-2).

10. Parlakian, R. and Lerner, C.. Beyond Twinkle, Twinkle: Using Music with Infants and Toddlers. The Performing Arts: Music, Dance, and Theater in the Early Years. Reprinted from Young Children March 2010. Pg 16-17.

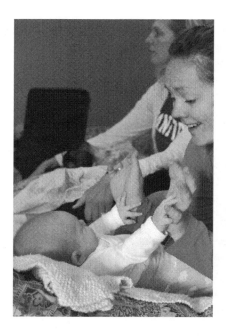

WHAT YOU CAN DO

Expose your baby to lots of different kinds of music, and watch how he reacts. He may share your musical preferences!

- **When choosing the music, think about:**

  ◦ Musical genre (Classical, Soul, Pop, Reggae, etc.)

  ◦ Instruments (a whole symphony, a violin, only a human voice/voices, etc.)

  ◦ Musical origin (is the song or artist from Western or Eastern culture?) – this may influence the tonality and/or the rhythm!

- **Play recorded music, but sing yourself, as well!**

  ◦ It doesn't matter if you can "carry a tune" – your baby will not judge your singing voice at this age

- ○ Your baby will benefit from the time he gets to focus on your mouth, your face, and the sounds coming out of your mouth

- *Great Resource:*

  - ○ Check out our Strength In Words podcast episodes **"Musical Patterns"** and **"Tips for Using Music to Support Development"**

9 WEEKS OLD: EARLIEST COMMUNICATION

Earliest Communication (Communicative Development)

In the first few weeks of your baby's life, crying was an unintentional, instinctual act to attract attention and meet her needs.

Assuming her crying *results* in your prompt response, from about 6 weeks of age, your baby has started to understand that if she cries, her needs will be met. In this way, the combination of crying and smiling become your baby's first "communicative" acts.

For the first three months, babies are using uncontrolled sounds with their mouths, such as tongue clicking, gurgling, burping, coughing, and vowel-like sounds. [11] Soon, these vowel sounds will shape more clearly into "cooing" sounds.

11. McLaughlin, S. (2006). Introduction to Language Development (2nd ed.). Clifton, NY: Thomson Delmar Learning.

WHAT YOU CAN DO

Respond to your baby! When she cries, let her know you are there for her (and do your best to give her what she needs).

- **Look into "Dunstan Baby Language"**

  - This system of reading the reflexive sounds your baby makes may help you learn to differentiate her cries in the first three months

- **When your baby is awake and alert, lie next to her or put your head close to hers and imitate her sounds, adding your own** [12]

  - The "best" sounds are language in action – hearing the sounds of your home language(s) is what allows her to

12. R. P. Cooper and others, "The Development of Infants' Preference for Motherese," Infant Behavior and Development 20, no. 4 (1997): 477–88.

catalogue information about speech sounds and language in general

- Every time you speak to her, you are teaching her more about human communication!

  ◦ That said, *any* sounds you make are great, because she can study the way your mouth moves, and the different qualities of all the sounds you make

- **Practice "taking turns"**

  ◦ When your baby makes a sound, imitate hers or make one of your own back to her, then stay quiet for several seconds or until she responds back

- **Remember that the sounds and "melody" of the language(s) you speak with your baby are helping her to form later understanding of speech and language** [13]

  ◦ Every time you speak to her, she learns more about language (and about you!)

- *Great Resource:*

  ◦ Check out our Strength In Words podcast episodes, **"Communication: The First 6 Months"** and **"Infant-Directed Speech"**

10 WEEKS OLD: EARLY TEXTURAL EXPERIENCE

Early Textural Experience (Motor Development)

---

13. L. Bloom and others, "Early Conversations and Word Learning: Contributions from Child and Adult," Child Development 67 (1996): 3154–75.

Newborns have automatic responses called "reflexes," which enable them to do various things instinctively.

By about 3-4 months or so, typically developing babies will start to *purposefully* attempt to reach and grasp objects with their hands. [14]

Before this, a young infant will hold onto an object if placed in his palm (this is called the *palmar grasp reflex*).

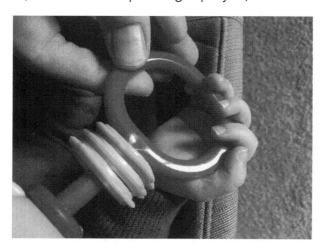

WHAT YOU CAN DO

Take advantage of the palmar grasp reflex, and place different kinds of objects in or near your baby's hand to allow her to experience various textures even though she isn't yet purposefully reach for items. [15]

- **Ideas include (but not limited to):**

  ◦ Your finger (human touch is like nothing else!)

14. Cratty, B.J. (1979). Perceptual and Motor Development in Infants and Children (2nd ed.). Englewood Cliffs, NJ: Prentice-Hall, Inc.
15. E. J. Gibson, "What Does Infant Perception Tell Us About Theories of Perception?," Journal of Experimental Psychology: Human Perception and Performance 13, no. 4 (1987): 515–23.

- ◦ Something soft (a blanket, sheepskin)
- ◦ Something that makes noise or rattles when knocked or moved (a shaker, a safely sealed bottle with rice inside)
- ◦ Something cool (a smooth rock) and something warm (a surface after it's been touched by a hot water bottle)
- ◦ Something different (sandpaper, a "dryer ball," something wooden, metal, plastic, or cardboard, etc.)

11 WEEKS OLD: ROUTINES AND RITUALS

Routines and Rituals (Social/Emotional Development)

It can be said that caregiving routines are often the most powerful opportunities for learning.[16] These are the experiences that happen regularly and consistently throughout the day.

Not only is your baby experiencing and participating (in her own way) in daily routines, she is also learning about interaction, and will eventually be able to predict what will come next as well as anticipate transitions from the end of one activity to the start of a new one.[17]

Traditionally, we think of daily routines for babies as events like waking up, going to sleep, eating/drinking (nursing/bottle, eventually solids), washing and bathing, dressing, diaper changing, etc.

16. Dunst, C.J., Bruder, M.B., Triftete, C.M., Raab, M., & McLean, M. (2001). Natural learning opportunities for infants, toddlers, and preschoolers. Young Exceptional Children, 4(3), 14-25.
17. Dunst, C.J., Hamby, D., Trivette, C.M., Raab, M., and Bruder, M.B. (2000). Everyday family and community life and children's naturally occurring learning opportunities. Journal of Early Intervention, 23(3), 151-164.

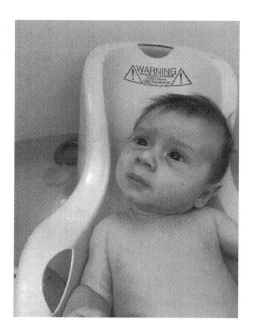

WHAT YOU CAN DO

Make these times special for you and your baby, and add other special moments throughout the day or to highlight different occasions to add "ritual" to your lives.

- **Sing a special song or say a phrase during each of those times**

  - It could be something you have heard or enjoyed, or something a family member said to you when you were small

  - When your baby wakes up to start the day, for instance, you might look out the window and sing a song (or talk) about the weather outside

  - Even saying something in a silly voice to prepare her for the next activity (such as, "stiiiinky diaper! It's tiiiiime for a new one!" will provide a consistent cue for her to learn what comes next and create a silly ritual shared by the two of you.

- **Add your own rituals**

  - These might be things you do daily, or things you do to mark special or rare occasions to "celebrate" different aspects of various events.

  - You might think about what you can do to transition from one part of the daily routine to the next (sing a song / say a silly rhyme about play time), or what special items you might bring out to help calm your baby if she gets a bump (a lavender pouch to place near her, a warmed pillow, a special picture book)

- *Great Resource:*

  - Check out the Strength In Words podcast episode, **"Routines and Rituals"**

12 WEEKS OLD: READ AND CLASSIFY

Read and Classify (Cognitive Development)

Classification (putting "like" things together) is a cognitive skill, and you can introduce activities or organize objects that are "themed" from very early on in your baby's life.

Your baby will enjoy spending time with you and listening to your voice, and will benefit from exposure to these organized activities by listening to the words you use.

Though this organization into categories is partially for the caregiver (it's nice to have a way to think about how to "present" activities for your baby!), research shows that babies as young as 3 months old start to show visual preference for basic categories of items they have seen before. This indicates that they are "storing" information about what they see from a very, very young age! [18]

WHAT YOU CAN DO

Decide on a few themes in which to organize items – a few you might start with might be: colors, shapes, animals, body parts

- **Use books that have something to do with that theme, or make your own with images from magazines (or printed web searches)**

  ○ *A note about this: PLEASE print images out instead of using*

18. Quinn, P.C., Eimas, P.D., Rosenkrantz, S.L. (1993). Evidence for representations of perceptually similar natural categories by 3-month-old and 4-month-old infants. Perception, 22, 463-475.

tablets or phones. The less we can promote the use of technology, at this age, the better! Sometimes, "low-tech" is better! For a more in-depth discussion of this issue, listen to the Strength In Words podcast episode, **"Building & Supporting Relationships."**

- **Use objects that relate to that theme**

  ◦ Dolls, toys, household items, or pictures/photographs

- **Read and talk about the things you have collected!**

  ◦ For ideas about what to say, think about answering some basic questions:

    ▪ What is the object you're looking at?

    ▪ What is its function? / How is it used?

    ▪ Where can you find it? / Where have you (and/or your baby) seen it before?

    ▪ Who has it, or one like it?

    ▪ When is it used? When have you seen it?

CHAPTER 2

Within this chapter, I'll suggest additional resources for you to explore on the Strength In Words website. You can find all of those resources organized by chapter here: https://www.strengthinwords.com/book-bonus

13 WEEKS OLD: INFANT MASSAGE

Infant Massage (Motor Development)

Body awareness is part of *perceptual motor development*, or the process of taking in, organizing and interpreting information that the body senses. [1]

Helping your baby start to understand where her body begins and ends through *touch* is a wonderful way to help her develop her perceptual motor skills.

1. Bertenthal, B.I. (1996). Origins and Early Development of Perception, Action and Representation. Annual Review of Psychology 47, 431-59.

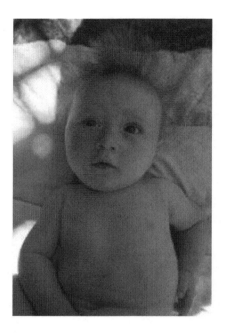

WHAT YOU CAN DO

There are many benefits to infant massage (especially for pre-term infants): it inherently promotes interaction between you and your baby,[2] it can calm your baby,[3] and it can help to reduce stress levels (for both of you)![4]

- **When your baby is relaxed and happy...**

  ○ Remove her clothes and diaper and lay her on a flat, comfortable surface (a mat, blanket, or sheepskin)

- **Look into her eyes and "ask" her if you can touch her**

2. Lee, H. (2006). The Effects of Infant Massage on Weight, Height, and Mother-Infant Interaction. Journal of Korean Academy of Nursing 36(8), 1331-1339.
3. Huhtala, V., Lehtonen, L., Heineken, R., Korvenranta, H. (2000). Infant Massage Compared With Crib Vibrator in the Treatment of Colicky Infants. Pediatrics 105(6).
4. Underdown, A., Barlow, J., Chung, V., Stewart-Brown, S. (2006). Massage intervention for promoting mental and physical health in infants aged under six months. The Cochrane Database of Systematic Reviews, Cd005038.

- Give her the chance to look back at you, wiggle in delight, smile, or react with other signals that you are learning to read as "positive"

- **Gently rub his legs, feet, arms and hands, stomach, neck, and forehead**

  - Try different kinds of light and (very) moderate pressure to see what she prefers. Some infants (and toddlers!) are calmed by different types of touch (light vs. deep pressure)

- **Create a calm and relaxing atmosphere**

  - Look into your baby's eyes, speak softly or sing a favorite song, try dimming the lights or using natural light only

  - You might tell her what part of her body you're "working" on, or what is coming next

- **You may choose to use an emollient, edible oil**

  - (Edible – in case your baby ingests some from her skin)

  - There are oils marketed as "infant massage oil" (which are, indeed, lovely!) but sunflower oil, for instance, can work just as well!

  - You might test the oil on her skin first by applying a small dollup on a patch of her skin

- **You can continue for as long as you and your baby are enjoying the activity!**

  - If your baby does not respond positively, simply try again another time

14 WEEKS OLD: RESPECT FOR BABY

Respect For Baby (Social/Emotional Development)

Infants learn to form expectations about how they'll be treated starting from very early in life. They learn how adults respond to their crying, smiling, and early sounds (cooing), and whether these communication attempts are valued by family members and other caregivers. [5]

When we as caregivers demonstrate to a baby that he is valued, we are showing him respect, in a sense. We respect and care about his needs and teach him to develop a sense of trust and security.

The first few months of life are often referred to as the "fourth trimester," as young infants are still very much dependent on the caregiver to fulfill physical needs. Some research suggests that in those early months especially, sensory experiences that mimic a "womb-like" environment (swaddling, "shushing," rocking, etc.) can help to calm very young infants. [6] Now that your baby is out of that period, however, your baby is starting to change: he iss becoming more aware of and more curious about the outside world. [7]

He is picking up more information everyday, and the more positive input you can give him, the more positive is his understanding of the world.

5. Lally, R. (2009). The Science and Psychology of Infant-Toddler Care: How an Understanding of Early Learning Has Transformed Child Care. Zero to Three.
6. Karp, H. (2012). The Happiest Baby on the Block. New York, NY: Bantam Books.
7. Gonzalez-Mena, J. (2007). What to Do for a Fussy Baby: A Problem-Solving Approach. Beyond the Journal: Young Children on the Web. National Association for the Education of Young Children. Pg 4.

WHAT YOU CAN DO

Perhaps most importantly, try to be aware of your own emotional responses in the presence of your baby. Your baby learns what respectful, appropriate expressions are through you as caregiver – your facial expressions, the tone of your voice, etc.

- **Try to be aware of (and when possible, avoid!) making negative observations about your baby, or about others in your presence, in front of him**

  - Even if you feel he is "too young" to understand!

- **Label your baby's emotions, or ask what he might be feeling when he has a strong reaction to something**

  - Hushing and shushing his cries were very effective in the early days, but now you might find that validating his emotions, giving words to his feelings, and speaking directly to him may do more to reassure him that his feelings are valued

- **Give your baby time to respond to you when you ask him**

a question or make a comment, to model good turn-taking skills

- ◦ In this way, you model that you'll be patient and wait for his response before moving on to another question

• **Talk to your baby about what is coming next in the day, what you'll be doing, and who you'll see.**

- ◦ Make her part of the process of the day

15 WEEKS OLD: TURN-TAKING

Turn-Taking (Communicative Development)

Babies start to become more interactive during this period, and typically start to use their voices to coo (using vowels such as "oo" and "ah") around the age of 3-4 months.

Your baby may smile and coo at you to express pleasure, request your attention, or to respond to something you said or did. [8]

8. McLaughlin, S. (2006). Introduction to Language Development (2nd ed.). Clifton, NY: Thomson Delmar Learning.

WHAT YOU CAN DO

When she communicates – with her voice, her facial expression, and/or her body, speak back to her.

- **You can imitate her sounds or movements, as well as speak about what she's doing**

  - Pause and wait for her to initiate again (she may do it sooner or may do it after several seconds)

  - In this way, you are engaging in a back-and-forth "conversation," taking turns as if you were talking with anyone else!

- **Sing a song or nursery rhyme, and when you finish, pause to watch what she does**

  - If you perceive that she wants you to continue the activity (i.e., she smiles, giggles, wiggles her extremities, looks directly into your eyes, coos to you, etc.)

  - You might say, "let's do it again!" In this way, you are modeling to her that you value her response, and can read what she communicates to you!

16 WEEKS OLD: EXPLORING PROPERTIES

Exploring Properties (Cognitive Development)

Around the age of four months, babies typically develop "binocular vision," allowing their eyes to work together and see *farther* than the previous 12-14 inches away (just far enough to look into a parent or caregiver's eyes from where he's sitting in your arms). [9]

9. Braddick, O. J., Atkinson, J., Julesz, B., Kropfl, W., Bodis-Wollner, I., & Raab, E. (1980). Cortical binocularity in infants. Nature, 288, 363–365.

This visual development, along with the development of more fine motor control with his fingers, allows your baby to delve into the world of reaching and grasping. As your baby's fine motor skills increase during this period (3-6 months and beyond), he will start to hold and transfer objects between his hands, and "play" with objects more purposefully. [10]

WHAT YOU CAN DO

You might organize a few (safe!) objects for your baby according to their "property" – find a few objects in your home that are "alike" in some way, and place them in a low bowl (a mixing bowl, a wooden basket) or on the floor next to him. This can be done during tummy time, or simply when lying on the floor on his back or side.

- **You might organize the objects by:**

  - Color, shape, texture, etc.

  - You might locate a variety of square(ish)-shaped objects (i.e., a book, a puzzle piece, a soap dish, and a small box)

10. Lewkowicz, D.J., Lickliter, R. (1994). The Development of Intersensory Perception: Comparative Perspectives. Hillsdale, NJ: Lawrence Erlbaum Associates, Inc.

- **Your baby may pick one out and inspect it**

  ◦ Watch how your baby engages with the object and talk about what he is doing

- **You might take out an object and model to your baby different ways to play with it (i.e., open and close a box, shake it to see if anything is inside, etc.)**

  ◦ All the while, narrate what you're doing

  ◦ Even if your baby does not readily imitate your play with the item, he will be "taking it in" and storing that information for later

- *Great Resource:*

  ◦ Check out a great example of how this can be done with our post, **"DIY Sensory & Vocabulary Bowl"** from the Strength In Words Blog

17 WEEKS OLD: REACH AND HOLD

Reach and Hold (Motor Development)

Typically, from 3-4 months of age, babies begin to reach out for things around them and soon attempt to hold onto these objects. This is a big step in your baby's development, as she is starting to move more purposefully.

Your baby will likely start by willfully swiping at objects that attract her attention (the beginning of "reaching"). As time goes on, the fingers and thumb begin to extend (independent of the whole hand) to sweep up objects, and flex to contain objects (the start of holding an object). [11]

11. von Hofsten, C. (1989). Mastering Reaching and Grasping: The Development of Manual Skills in Infancy. Advances in Psychology, 61, 223-258.

Your baby will likely bring an object she has grasped up to her mouth – this is because "oral exploration" is a natural early developmental stage, wherein your baby is able to discover the taste and texture of different objects.

WHAT YOU CAN DO

When she is content to play, introduce various objects in her immediate environment and at different levels; for instance, things she can see on her tummy, on her back, on the wall beside her, directly above her, and slightly out of reach.

- **Try presenting a new toy by modeling what** *you* **might do with it**

  ◦ First demonstrate, yourself. She may or may not follow suit – for instance, if you shake a rattle or bang on a drum, she may do the same or may simply grab and mouth the object

- ◦ Either way, she is exploring and learning (she also may not be interested in that object, which is perfectly acceptable! She is developing her own preferences!

- **Give her experience with objects that:**

  - ◦ Vary in color, texture, size, shape, or that make various sounds when you touch them (such as an egg shaker or a rattle)

  - ◦ As she touches these objects, talk about what is different or similar about each of them

- **Give her a chance to attempt purposeful movement!**

  - ◦ It can be tempting to bring her hand to an object to "help" her interact with it, but if you allow her to attempt things herself at her own pace, you might be surprised by what she can do herself!

  - ◦ Blowing bubbles can be a wonderfully interactive activity

    - ▪ Your baby might attempt to "pop" a bubble *herself* if you bring it close to her

18 WEEKS OLD: JOINT ATTENTION

Joint Attention (Communicative Development)

As babies begin to become more interactive, they start to develop social awareness, paying attention not only to an object in front of them, but also to *how* their caregiver is engaging with that object. They begin to engage in what is known as joint attention. This is, essentially, the shared attention between two people interacting with each other and with an object (it could be your hands, a puppet, a plane in the sky that your baby looks at, etc.) For a discussion of joint attention, please listen to the Strength In Words podcast episode, **"Why Sing?"**

A "sister" to joint attention is joint reference. This refers to the going back and forth between the object and person – through your gaze, words, and gestures, you refer to each other and to the object.

Joint attention is also a part of learning the skill of taking turns, in that each of the "communication partners" (you and your baby) is looking to the other for a communicative purpose (perhaps for acknowledgment, to comment, to affirm or negate, etc.), and when that message is received by one, it's up to the other person to continue the conversation! [12]

12. Mundy, P., Newell, L. (2007). Attention, Joint Attention, and Social Cognition. Current Directions in Psychological Sciences, 16(5): 269-274.

WHAT YOU CAN DO

Create lots of interactive shared experiences. In real life, this translates in basic everyday activities that you share with your baby (caregiving routines like diapering, feeding, bath time, etc. as well as short play activities)

- **Talk about what you're doing, what you see where you are**
- **Respond to your baby's:**

  - *Gaze* (by following it, commenting on it)
  - *Gesture* (say the word aloud for what she's pointing to, and expend, guessing based on context whether she's making a request, commenting, or something else)
  - *Vocalization* (did it sound like a word? Was she playing with her voice? Assuming that she used her voice to communicate something, regardless of whether it was a specific idea or simply a feeling, and talk about what you think she might be saying, and why!)
  - *Expand*, expand, expand the conversation!

- **Model joint referencing**

  - If you're referring to something nearby, use gestures (like pointing), and look back and forth between the object/person and your baby

- **Other natural activities that promote joint attention:**

  - Reading
  - Sitting together (for instance, looking out the window)
  - Laying together and looking together at something with which your baby is already engaged

- ◦ Blowing bubbles
- ◦ Using puppets

19 WEEKS OLD: EARLY LITERACY

Early Literacy (Communicative Development)

It is *never* too early to expose your child to early literacy skills! It's important to recognize that the term "early literacy" is not the same thing as "learning how to read." [13]

When you read to / with your baby, you are teaching him about joint attention, described in last week's activity. You create an interactive, shared experience.

When reading to your baby, you expose him to text – and highlight its importance in our lives.

WHAT YOU CAN DO

---

13. Schickedanz, J.A. (1999). Much More than the ABCs: The Early Stages of Reading and Writing. Washington, D.C.: NAEYC.

No book is "too advanced" for your baby if used appropriately! In the early months, it's not as much about content as it is about your baby hearing your voice, feeling close to you, and watching (and being part of) what you're doing and how you interact with the world.

- **You might read a page and point to a picture, then look at and say to your baby, "look at that fish! See the fish?"**

  - Even very young babies (if caught in the right moment) will look at the pictures, look at you, then look again toward the book – as if to say, "Yes, I see it! Let's look more!"

- **Encourage your baby to engage directly and appropriately with books.**

  - If your baby reaches out to touch a book, encourage her to "turn the page," – even if that simply means that you move the page towards her hand to tempt her to reach out and touch it!

- **Read using lots of animated voices to help keep her attention**

  - Let her hear you play with your voice – she'll start doing the same once she starts to coo, shriek, blow raspberries, and babble!

- **Point to different objects and characters on the page (if there are pictures) and name them**

  - Talk *also* about what the characters are doing, what time of day/season, etc.

  - Don't be confined by the text on the page

- *Great Resource:*

○ Don't miss the Strength In Words podcast episode, **"How to Provide Early Literacy Experiences for Infants and Toddlers"** for great ideas from our guest Kayla O'Neill, an early interventionist

20 WEEKS OLD: PHOTOGRAPHS

Photographs (Social/Emotional Development)

Part of your baby's social/emotional development includes his ability to establish positive relationship with others – both adults and peers. [14]

Young babies often prefer to look at people (over objects) [15] and, when alert and calm, are very much interested in engaging socially.

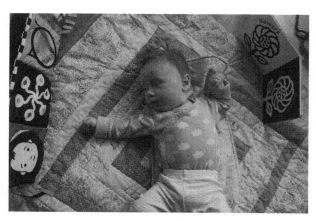

WHAT YOU CAN DO

14. Saskatchewan Ministry of Education, Early Learning and Child Care Branch Ministry of Education Fall 2010. Play and Exploration for Infants and Toddlers: A Companion Booklet to Play and Exploration: Early Learning Program Guide. www.education.gov.sk.ca/ELCC. Pg 12.
15. M. H. Johnson and others, "Newborns' Preferential Tracking of Face-Like Stimuli and Its Subsequent Decline," Cognition 40, no. 1-2 (1991): 1-19.

Collect a few favorite photographs of family, friends, and/or departed loved ones, and put them in a baby-friendly "photo album" or collection of pocket sheet protector pages – anything that your baby can easily look at, or hold and touch or mouth without completely destroying the integrity of the photo.

- **Use this as an opportunity to talk about those people, and integrate those who have passed on**
- **Tell the story of what is happening in the photograph**

  ◦ Answer your own who, what, where, when, why questions to keep you talking

- **Alternatively:**

  ◦ Find images of animals, nature objects, even interesting textures or colors (in old magazines, from a printed web search)

  ◦ Post them in your home (at baby's level!) and use this as an opportunity to talk about what you see

  ◦ This may be a nice option to have on the wall next to a diaper-changing station

- *Great Resource:*

  ◦ Check out the Strength In Words episode, "**Bringing Montessori Home**" for additional Montessori-inspired ideas from our guest, Jeanne-Marie Paynel, a Montessori Consultant

21 WEEKS OLD: CHOICE-MAKING

Choice-Making (Cognitive Development)

Your baby is starting to make purposeful movements, and is also beginning to make rudimentary choices or decisions during play. She will decide which toy to pick up, and will study it in various ways (often, this will be primarily oral exploration)! [16]

Allowing your baby to make a choice not only gives her the feeling that she has a say in what happens in her life, but also creates additional opportunities for back and forth communication between you – she "chooses" something, and you read her response, validating her purposeful communication and her ability to make a decision.

WHAT YOU CAN DO

Give your baby choices whenever you can! It may be easier (for her and for you) to present two choices at a time.

- **You may read her non-verbal responses to your options by looking at:**

  ○ Her gaze – it may linger at one object after she looks between the two, or she may only focus on one

16. California Department of Education, California Infant/Toddler Curriculum Framework, Sacramento, 2012, pg. 105.

- ◦ Her gesture – she may reach for one or move her body towards one of them

- **When you see her "choose" one, give her feedback about what you saw**

  - ◦ "I saw you look at this one! Sure, let's do that!"

  - ◦ If she grabs both of them, there are a few options... accept that she would like both (when appropriate), take one for yourself and one for her to play with (so you are playing with both together), or take a moment to see which one she is more focused on

- **If your baby appears overwhelmed by a number of choices (i.e., a boxful of toys):**

  - ◦ Take two out and present them, one in each hand

- **As part of a bedtime routine:**

  - ◦ Present two book options to her so she can choose which book to read (or in which order to read them)

- **When you are dressing your baby:**

  - ◦ You might give her a choice of which clothing item to wear

- *Great Resource:*

  - ◦ Don't miss our choice-making activity using simple objects,**"DIY Animal Images"** from the Strength In Words DIY Blog!

22 WEEKS OLD: TUMMY AND TURN

Tummy and Turn (Motor Development)

Continue to give your baby opportunities to spend supervised time on his tummy, as this helps him develop muscles (primarily those in his neck and trunk).

As he learns to move in different ways – on his back, his belly, and turning from one to the other – he learns to explore and problem-solve.

Rather than age as the best predictor of when babies will reach gross motor milestones, more recent studies indicate that *experience* may be the strongest predictor of later milestones such as crawling and walking. [17] [18]

WHAT YOU CAN DO

17. Adolph, K. E., Joh, A. S. (2007). "Motor Development: How Infants Get Into the Act," in Introduction to Infant Development (2nd ed.), edited by A. Slater and M. Lewis; New York: Oxford University Press.
18. Adolph, K.E., Vereijken, B., Shrout, P. E. (2003). "What Changes in Infant Walking and Why," Child Development 74(2), 475–497.

Lie down facing your baby on your belly so you are on his level. Talk about or play with other objects that you might put in his vicinity, such as baby-safe mirrors, fabric books, rattles, etc.

- **Rather than using equipment to "assist" your baby to develop, create a safe play space on the floor that is non-restrictive**

  ◦ Allow him to enjoy his natural movements, exploration, and learning about his environment

  ◦ *This* is the type of "experience" that will encourage him to reach, roll, and crawl

- **Encouraging your baby to move freely is also part of respecting his own initiative**

  ◦ Rather than handing him a toy, you might place several within or just out of reach

  ◦ Watch to see which one he chooses, or how he problem solves how to reach it

23 WEEKS OLD: OBSERVING MUSICAL DIFFERENCES

Observing Musical Differences (Cognitive Development)

Young babies can be given the opportunity to observe differences in instrument sounds and different types of music with variations in rhythm, pitch, and tonality.

Infants within this age range (3-6 months) are often partial to the interactive nature of a caregiver singing directly to them. [19]

19. Parlakian, R. and Lerner, C.. Beyond Twinkle, Twinkle: Using Music with Infants and Toddlers. The Performing Arts: Music, Dance, and Theater in the Early Years. Reprinted from Young Children March 2010. Pg 16-18.

WHAT YOU CAN DO

Give your baby the opportunity to both listen to various types of music (live and recorded), and also to play with creating different sounds herself.

- **When you sing to your baby, play with the words and adjust them to your needs**

  - For instance, a song that is usually about brushing teeth can become a song about driving in a car.

  - Start to use familiar tunes with unfamiliar words (repetition with variation) to keep your baby interested and expose her to familiar vocabulary in a new context.

- **Provide your baby with a number of instruments that vary in the type of sounds she can make.**

  - She may focus on simply moving the instruments to make the sound (cause and effect), or she may inspect it to figure out how it works.

  - Feeling it in and around her mouth may be a major part of understanding the object's texture, shape, size, etc.

- **Young babies will often enjoy handling instruments such as egg shakers, maracas, bells and drums**

  - The same types of objects can easily be made at home with beans/grains/kernels placed in safely sealed containers or with upside down pots, pans, plastic or metal bowls, etc.

- *Great Resource:*

  - For a "how to" round up of all Strength In Words' DIY instruments, please check out our **"DIY Family Band"** post and the corresponding podcast episode, **"Happiness & Relationships,"** for an example of how we use them in song.

24 WEEKS OLD: PUPPETS

Puppets (Social/Emotional Development)

At this young age, building relationships, interacting with others, and building an identity of self in relation to others are all crucial components of social and emotional development.

Care routines (such as diapering, eating, dressing, bathing, bathing, etc.) are more emotionally satisfying for your baby when there is interaction and participation on both your parts. [20]

---

20. California Department of Education, California Infant/Toddler Curriculum Framework, Sacramento, 2012, pg. 66.

WHAT YOU CAN DO

Puppets can be a useful tool to encourage creative play and vocabulary development – and can be great for you as a parent to help you feel comfortable being silly!

- **Puppets come in all shapes and sizes**

  ◦ They can provide an entertaining distractor for little hands to reach and hold as your baby becomes more wiggly and mobile!

- **Puppets can take any form or be made from any material**

  ◦ They can be soft and cuddly animals / people / objects

  ◦ Made from a paper bag (colored, decorated with a face), a sock or stocking, a glove...

- **Use them to focus on or talk about specific vocabulary, such as body parts or action words**

  - The puppet can point to its own body parts or your baby's, or can act out actions (like crawling or dancing)

- **Make them a part of a reading activity**

  - They can act out parts of the story or be the character in the story

- **Help baby to stay entertained**

  - While on the go, you can use smaller finger puppets in the stroller, car, public transportation

  - Play peek-a-boo, sing silly songs, dance and do finger plays

- *Great Resource:*

  - Check out our **"DIY Dishwashing Glove Puppet"** from the Strength In Words DIY Blog!

CHAPTER 3

Within this chapter, I'll suggest additional resources for you to explore on the Strength In Words website. You can find all of those resources organized by chapter here: https://www.strengthinwords.com/book-bonus

25 WEEKS OLD: BABBLE AND GESTURE

Babble and Gesture (Communicative Development)

Typically, somewhere between 4 and 10 months, babies start to use "vocal play" in the form of babbling. Babbling (vs. the earlier "cooing,") refers to the sounds babies make when they start to use consonants.

Initially, your baby will likely use one sound in isolation, and then put together consonant-vowel combinations. As he plays with the sounds his mouth makes (and watches and listens to you forming words), he will start to use more varying consonants and vowels, his sounds becoming more complex. [1]

There is research to suggest that rhythmic arm activity (e.g., banging) increases substantially at the same time as the onset

1. McLaughlin, S. (2006). Introduction to Language Development (2nd ed.). Clifton, NY: Thomson Delmar Learning.

of babbling, and that there is a relationship between infant gesture and the acquisition of spoken language. [2]

WHAT YOU CAN DO

You can encourage your baby to make these sounds by speaking to him, as you have been doing, but also singing using sounds like "ba" or "ma" (without worrying about using actual words), or simply by making simple sounds and "playing" with your voice in consonant-vowel combination to break down the elements, getting close to him and saying, "ba-ba-ba," "da-da-da," "ma-ma-ma," etc. As time goes on, your baby will start to babble not only to stimulate himself, but also for a social purpose: he will learn that when he speaks, he will be reinforced by you, the caregiver!

- **If gesture, movement and language development all influence each other, it stands to reason that the more face-to-face, social and meaningful activity you participate in with your baby, the more he can benefit!**

  ○ *Play Peek-a-boo!* He's watching your hands, your eyes, your

2. Iverson, J. M., Hall, A. J., Nickel, L., & Wozniak, R. H. (2007). The Relationship between Reduplicated Babble Onset and Laterality Biases in Infant Rhythmic Arm Movements. Brain and Language, 101(3), 198–207.

face, and at some point soon, will find it amazing and hilarious that you're still there even when your face is covered (part of "object permanence," which we'll talk about more another week)

- *Play with rhythm* (tapping your hand on your knee or on his, to the beat of a song) and perform finger plays, which often rhyme and have their own rhythm (or meter)

- *Encourage waving hello and good-bye* – mostly by modeling it yourself when you are greeting others, instead of grabbing his hand and doing it for him (he'll imitate when he's ready, and when it's meaningful to him!)

- *Bang on kitchen items / utensils / drums / shakers* of any sort! Make rhythms together and *copy* the sounds he makes, having a "rhythmic conversation" of sorts

- *Great Resource:*

  - For a broader discussion of this topic and auditory examples of how to maximize play, listen to the Strength In Words podcast episode, **"How To Respond To Your Babbling Baby"**

26 WEEKS OLD: VISUAL SCAN AND REACH

Visual Scan and Reach (Motor Development)

Physical and motor development refer to the development of all "motor" skills, or movements of the body – involving the large and small muscles. This includes movements of the eyes, and your baby's growing ability to look at and study (or "visually scan") items in front of her. Now, her eye and hand skills are able to start working together in a more fine-tuned manner.

As your baby learns to control the large and small muscles of her body, she is also learning about the *items* in her environment that she is able to manipulate.

Research suggests that infants around the age of 6 months begin to use information they take in visually to guide their physical actions. She adjusts her movements (reaching, grasping, etc.) according to visual-spatial cues, and uses this information to help her determine what she wants to do with objects she's found.[3]

Your baby is starting to integrate aspects of visual information to determine *how* she can manipulate something, or *what* she might do with it – taking in what she's seen before (whether it was you stirring a spoon in a bowl, or recalling what happened to a sand castle when she put her hand down into it, etc.), and applying that information to new experiences, experimenting with her own behavior and impact on the world. From 6 months, your baby may be starting to use her own senses to guide her behavior, suggesting that *giving her time to learn without interfering in her own choices about what and how to play with objects* is essential.

3. Claxton, L., Keen, J., R., McCarty, M. E. (2003). Evidence of Motor Planning in Infant Reaching Behavior. Psychological Science 14 (4). 354–56.

WHAT YOU CAN DO

Give her access to a few objects at a time so she can choose what interests her, and try to offer objects that vary in texture, quality, size, shape, etc.

- **Use an empty egg carton**

  ◦ Using a half or whole dozen carton, fill a few of (or all of) the spaces with household or play objects (i.e., a ball of scrunched up paper, a sock, a puzzle piece, a ball, a rattle)

  ◦ Egg cartons can be easily manipulated by a young baby, and she may even be able to open it herself

- **Create a "sensory bag"**

  ◦ You can use a clear plastic sealable bag (making sure it is really sealed, and adding an additional seal with tape if you like)

- ○ Add food coloring to water or shaving cream to make it a colorful experience, or keep it clear and add small plastic objects (i.e., buttons, beads, plastic animals) or food objects (i.e., grapes, berries, ice cubes), or any variation you can think of!

- **Offer a "sensory bin"**

  - ○ Place objects inside that she can grab out of a shallow bowl or box

  - ○ You can group them by some similar quality that each of the objects share (whether by a physical quality or their functional use) to add to the things you might say about them, and to help suggest to her the idea of categories.

27 WEEKS OLD: PUT IN, TAKE OUT

Put In, Take Out (Motor Development)

As your baby starts to sit upright (either independently or with your body as a support), he will soon be able to access objects from new angles and perspectives. Simultaneously, he will be working on his ability to grab hold of objects, and will become more adept at exploring in different ways (including use of his mouth)! [4]

Your baby learns through the process of repetition – repeating similar actions allows him to practice moving his body in certain ways, or problem-solve how to get from one place to another... including getting *into* something!

---

4. von Hofsten, C. (1989). Mastering Reaching and Grasping: The Development of Manual Skills in Infancy. Advances in Psychology, 61, 223-258.

Manipulating objects (moving them around, exploring how they work and what they do) is an early part of learning about orientation skills – which sets the foundation for other visual motor skills she will develop later on (such as writing, building the logic to complete puzzles, etc). [5]

He will likely learn to take things out before he learns to put them back in, so you as caregiver can model for him how to reload and repeat the activity until he can do (or is interested in doing) it himself.

WHAT YOU CAN DO

Offering containers that can be easily opened or that have openings on one side can allow him to explore what is inside, and help him develop the skills to problem solve, remember what he did the last time, and understand how to move in order to get something out.

- **Use a 3-sided or rounded container**

  - This might be a shoebox, low plastic bin, a wicker basket, a mixing bowl...

5. MacDonald, M., Lipscomb, S., McClelland, M. M., Duncan, R., Becker, D., Anderson, K., & Kile, M. (2016). Relations of Preschoolers' Visual-Motor and Object Manipulation Skills With Executive Function and Social Behavior. Research Quarterly for Exercise and Sport, 1-12.

- Place objects inside, and allow your baby to take things out – one at a time or all at once!

- **Use a closed shoebox with a hand-sized hole cut through the top, or a tissue box**

  - He must turn the container, shake, or reach in to get things out

- **Use a box that is closed, but that he can open independently**

  - A nesting toy, a "nearly" peeled off lid on a canister, etc.
  - Shake this toy while you sing a song to him
  - Hide different objects inside, and when the song is over, offer the container to him as a temptation to remove the lid and see what's inside!
  - Listen to the *Strength In Words* podcast, **"Visual Supports, An Intro,"** to hear this at work!

- **When he has finished playing with a particular toy (either he has taken all the objects out of the box, or he has become bored)**

  - Model putting things away by making this its *own* activity
    - Each toy that goes back in the box can come with a silly song,
    - Each toy that goes back comes with the the word *"in"*
    - Each toy that goes back gets a sing-song voice saying "good-bye!"
  - You might hand him one of the objects and place the container in front of him, pausing expectantly.

◦ If he doesn't drop it in, you can "help" him to show him what you expect, and then sing/say the same silly sound when he has completed the action.

28 WEEKS OLD: SOCIAL AWARENESS

Social Awareness (Social/Emotional Development)

Typically, babies within this age range start to watch or become aware of other children in the group around the time when they are able to sit up and look around.

They begin to show more of an interest in what others are playing with, and how other people (both children *and* adults) engage with objects – the beginning of a more interactional stage that includes more imitation and engagement between peers and with adults. [6]

WHAT YOU CAN DO

6. Striano, T., Rochat, P. (2000). Emergence of Selective Social Referencing in Infancy. Infancy 1(2), 253–64.

Give your baby the opportunity to play with others around her age when possible and play "social games" with her yourself.

- **Social games include things like peek-a-boo, reading or rhythmically chanting nursery rhymes, and singing songs**

    ◦ At times, try to include a prop of some kind (a musical instrument, a colorful scarf, a puppet) so that she can watch how you use the object

    ◦ She may attempt to imitate you, or she may simply observe you (or be busy with something else!!)

    ◦ Try to respect her desire and allow her to engage freely in the activity (instead of directing her to do specific things)

- **When your baby is playing around other peers, whether in an adult-led group or a non-structured play setting, try to allow her the space and freedom to learn on her own as much as possible**

    ◦ Resist the urge to manipulate her hands

    ◦ Remember to give her time to explore her surroundings on her own before you intervene

    ◦ This allows her to develop confidence in herself, and start to learn the social rules of her environment on her own

- **This is not an age that you can reasonably expect your baby to "share" (the reality is that this doesn't come for a few more YEARS)**

    ◦ In addition, she is still developing the fine motor skills to become 'gentle' (though encouraging soft touches instead of grabbing or hitting may be a good way to familiarize her with this concept and increase her awareness of others)

○ If your baby takes something from another child (or vice versa) and you feel the need to intervene, you might offer another option to the baby who's lost the object, or give a choice of other (potentially similar) objects to your baby (or to whoever "the taker" is)

29 WEEKS OLD: PAINTING AND PLAYING

Painting and Playing (Motor Development)

As solids are introduced and purposeful movements are further developing, your baby may enjoy experiencing and experimenting with different textures.

To give your baby the opportunity to create and "be messy," edible and/or washable paint can be a wonderful way to introduce your baby to the idea of artistic expression – in the form of color, texture and movement – with the added benefit of taste exploration!

At this age and stage, "playing with your food" is a *completely* natural and positive way for your baby to experience food. Introducing foods in a play situation allows young children to interact with and familiarize themselves with new foods, experience it using other senses (smell, texture, visual, etc.) and can remove anxiety of actually eating (especially for any little ones with food aversions or sensory issues). [7]

---

7. Douglas, J. (2002), Psychological Treatment of Food Refusal in Young Children. Child and Adolescent Mental Health, 7: 173–180.

WHAT YOU CAN DO

Experiment with a variety of edible "finger painting" options offered in different locations and on a variety of surfaces!

- **Use a wipeable (or hose-able) surface**

  - Your options are really endless – a plastic tray, a bathtub, a table cloth, a porch, a tarp, a bowl, a large piece of paper...

- **Offer tools**

  - Your baby may want to use a spoon, a basting brush, or a sponge instead of her fingers, or in addition to them

  - You can model for her some ideas for how to use them, but try to let her figure out *whether* she wants to use them, and/or how

  - He may *only* want to play with the tools (rather than the paint!) which is ok, too!

  - Remember that the texture or temperature of paint may simply be a sensory experience she's not interested in at the moment

- **Baby-safe finger paints can be made by:**

  - Pureeing variously colored foods (think kiwi, strawberry, banana, cooked sweet potato, etc. – especially those that are overripe!

  - Mixing food coloring or natural dyes with cornstarch, flour, or yogurt

  - Listen to the Strength In Words podcast episode, **"What's So Great About Messy Play?"** and the corresponding DIY Blog post, **"DIY Edible Finger Paint & Sensory Play"** for further ideas and explanation

  - There is a great collection of ideas on the *Strength In Words* Pinterest board, **Infant/Toddler DIY Finger Painting**

- **For babies who are not at all interested in the sensory aspect of messy finger painting, there are alternatives:**

  - Place a few dollops of color on a piece of paper enclosed in a plastic bag, or inside a (sealed) sheet protector to allow them to see the color move as they touch it

30 WEEKS OLD: ANTICIPATION GAMES

Anticipation Games (Cognitive Development)

Personal care routines (i.e., diapering, feeding, eating, dressing/undressing, washing, etc.) provide a predictable sequence of events, and allow infants of this age to learn to anticipate next steps. The actions we do day in and day out help your baby to develop the memory and understanding of what comes next, allowing them to hone their natural desire to imitate our actions.

Since babies learn through repetition, [8] they often find repeated actions to be entertaining or interesting. This is part of why games like peek-a-boo, or song and finger plays, can be so much fun played over and over (and over) again.

WHAT YOU CAN DO

Play with the tempo/pace of familiar routines, songs/rhymes, or games that you play together, to keep your baby "on her toes" – this may keep her engaged for a longer time, and will call attention to different aspects of the activity than those she may have attended to previously!

- **While dressing:**

  - Instead of simply putting on a sock, make a "zoooooooooom"-ing sound and slowly bring the sock closer until you put it on

- **When singing a song:**

  - Pause (or elongate a pause) in the song to highlight

8. California Department of Education, California Infant/Toddler Curriculum Framework, Sacramento, 2012, pg. 105-106.

something that is about to happen – you may see her watching you expectantly!

- **When playing peek-a-boo:**
  - Vary the amount of time before you "reappear" so she doesn't know quite when to expect you
- **Create a new simple game:**
  - Hold a piece of fabric (any small clothing item) above her, wiggling it about, and drop it down on top of her body when she least expects it
  - Start to make a noise and move your body slowly toward hers as your vocalization gets louder until you suddenly tickle her body!

31 WEEKS OLD: GRASPING

Grasping (Motor Development)

The palmar grasp reflex (when something is placed in the baby's hand, the hand reflexively closes – a reflex we are born with) typically disappears by about 5 months of age. Around 3-5 months, babies typically begin to consciously grasp objects with their fingers.

Your baby will start his journey into purposeful grasping by swatting, then grabbing with his whole hand and "raking" something toward him or into the other hand, and eventually using more precise movements and parts of his hand. [9]

The ability to pick something up with one's forefinger and

9. Adolph, K. E., Joh, A. S. (2007). "Motor Development: How Infants Get Into the Act," in Introduction to Infant Development (2nd ed.), edited by A. Slater and M. Lewis; New York: Oxford University Press.

thumb (and then place the object in a controlled manner) is the use of the pincer grasp, and is typically mastered somewhere around 9-10 months. This is a time that lots of hand-eye coordination is developing. One of the most common uses of the pincer grasp for a baby of this age is related to eating solids, as it allows him to feed himself smaller bits in a more refined way.

WHAT YOU CAN DO

Give your baby lots of opportunities to grasp and hold objects, presenting just a few at a time so he's able to focus (and therefore more likely to experiment with an object).

- **Play with objects that can be separated, and/or can be held all at once**

  - Scarves, cooked pasta, tissues in a box, etc.

- **Give him the opportunity to explore smaller toys (under your focused supervision!) so he can practice grasping and picking up objects of different shapes and sizes**

- Kitchen items (i.e., spoons, metal / plastic / wooden bowls or cups)
- Blocks
- Toy cars or animal figurines
- Instruments

- **Provide soft finger foods that your baby can feed himself**

  - Such as roasted vegetables, slices of soft fruit, strips of bread, cereal "O's, etc.
  - For more information and ideas, you might consider looking into "Baby Led Weaning/Eating"

32 WEEKS OLD: ATTACH AND EXPLORE

Attach and Explore (Social/Emotional Development)

From the very beginning, babies seek security – *especially* up through the age of around 9 months. From around this time, typically developing babies are often beginning to become more mobile (with skills that are slowly emerging or they are quickly mastering – the spectrum is broad!), and their focus becomes more about exploration of the environment *further* away from the caregiver. [10]

The security your baby has developed by being able to rely on and and trust her caregivers to be predictably responsive to her needs allows her the confidence to know that, if she leaves your side to momentarily explore the environment, you will be there when she needs you again. This knowledge enables her to continue to form her own identity and sense of self. [11]

10. Zero to Three. (2008). Caring for infants & toddlers in groups: Developmentally appropriate practice (2nd ed.). Washington, DC: Zero to Three.
11. Shonkoff, J.P., & D.A. Phillips, eds. 2000. From neurons to neighborhoods: The science of

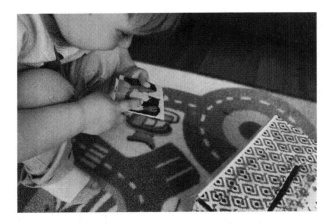

WHAT YOU CAN DO

"Engineer" parts of your home environment to provide materials that support relationships between your baby and you, your partner, other familiar adults, as well as frequently seen children (siblings, cousins, friends).

- **Include pictures of these important people**

  ◦ Place them in accessible areas of your home, in photo albums, in sheet protectors, or laminated on cardstock/cardboard

- **Include pictures of familiar places or activities**

  ◦ When your baby takes an interest in these pictures, tell her about the last time she was there, what she did, who she was with, something special that happened, etc.

- **Embed pictures of people within her play materials**

  ◦ Place pictures of people on the underside of puzzle pieces that she can easily manipulate

early child development. A report of the National Research Council. Washington, DC: National Academies Press.

- Place them under a stacking block
- Place them inside a sack, so she (or you) can fish them out
- Make a game of finding the pictures, taking turns, or playing peek-a-boo with them!
- *To see this idea in action, visit the following Strength In Words DIY Blog posts:*
  - **"DIY Photo Mailbox"**
  - **"DIY Creative Puzzle Games"**

33 WEEKS OLD: SEPARATION ANXIETY

Separation Anxiety (Social/Emotional Development)

By the age of around 8 months, babies develop a rudimentary understanding of "object permanence," or the knowledge that objects and people exist even when not in view.

When a familiar adult disappears, your baby knows you are gone, but doesn't know where you've gone or when you'll come back! This can, understandably, create a sense of panic in your little one, and, for many babies, can lead to the appearance of a more clingy, "needy," child as his 1-year birthday approaches. It is important to remember that this shift is an important and healthy part of his social/emotional and cognitive development.

Experts in early childhood development and education typically agree that if you are leaving for any "real" period of time (dropping her off at daycare or leaving her with another caregiver to run errands/have some time for yourself), it's best to say a quick good-bye instead of simply disappearing. [12] [13] This

12. Bronson, M.B. (2000). Self-regulation in early childhood: Nature and nurture. New York: Guilford.
13. Pnina S. Klein, Ravit R. Kraft & Cilly Shohet (2008) Behaviour patterns in daily mother–child

creates consistency and allows her to learn to recognize that good-byes are an important social routine, and that she can depend on your cues to anticipate what is coming next.

WHAT YOU CAN DO

Help your baby understand that you have not left "for good."

- **If you're simply going into the next room, keep telling and telling her what you're doing and where you're going.**

  ○ Even if she cries, the sound of your voice will have a soothing effect overall!

- **Make sure there are nice reminders of you and other**

separations: possible opportunities for stress reduction, Early Child Development and Care,180:3, 387-396

familiar people in her environment when you are not present.

- This can take the form of photographs, familiar routines or activities that help her learn that her world will go on with some familiarity, even if you are not there in that moment.

- **Create a photo album featuring you and any other primary caregivers doing fun things your baby enjoys.**

  - On one side, feature a photograph; on the other side, a description of the scene, answering:

    - Who / What / When / Where / Why questions to serve as prompts

  - This can be taken out at any time (whether you are present or not), but can be a wonderful way for a new or less familiar caregiver to talk about you

  - It can also serve as a prompt for *distraction*: "Wow, here you are with your daddy playing with your stuffed animals! Let's play with them together, now! Can you show me?"

  - For a "how-to" of this activity, see the Strength In Words DIY Blog post, **"Familiar Family Book"**

- **Make a habit of playing games like "peek-a-boo"**

  - These games help her develop an appreciation for, and familiarize her with the fact that we are here even when hidden!

  - This is not to say that it will ease separation anxiety each time you leave, but it helps give her the tools to understand the concept as a whole.

- **Increase your baby's awareness of, and familiarity with, the fact that objects out of sight still exist**

  ◦ Place items into a container (bag, bucket, cardboard box, etc.), and peek inside, acting excited, to tempt your baby to reach in

  ◦ Explore the contents together

34 WEEKS OLD: SELF-EDUCATION IN MOVEMENT

Self-Education in Movement (Motor Development)

We know that babies learn about their bodies (the way they feel and move) by moving them – exploring their environment by rolling, sitting, scooting, falling, and feeling the sensation of another person touching them.

Research suggests that allowing babies to move freely positively influences their development and learning. [14] [15]Allowing your baby to learn on her own can mean giving her the space to learn new skills for herself, with your gentle encouragement.

A rule of thumb when thinking about motor skills typically acquired during this age range (such as sitting, crawling, and even walking) is that the process of your baby getting into a position is more important developmentally than being in that position [16] – that process is precisely how he learns, by problem

14. Sensory Awareness Foundation. 1994. Emmi Pikler. Sensory Awareness Bulletin 14.
15. California Department of Education, California Infant/Toddler Curriculum Framework, Sacramento, 2012, pg. 127.
16. Gonzalez-Mena, J. & Eyer, D. W. (2003). Infants, Toddlers, and Caregivers: A Curriculum of Respectful, Responsive Care and Education, 6th ed. New York: McGraw-Hill Companies.

solving, feeling supported by you, listening to your voice, and finding new ways to move his body as it grows and strengthens.

WHAT YOU CAN DO

Give your baby access to materials that support perceptual and motor development, and that focus on his interests.

- Place objects of interest in places he can manipulate them

  - Placed on the floor, or on a low table if he is starting to hoist himself up to access items

  - Use items like puzzles, pictures, dolls, books, empty paper roll holders, or musical instruments

- Consider hanging a mirror at a low level so he can watch himself move

- As he starts to scoot or crawl, create different surfaces for him on the floor

  - For instance, a mat, a pillow, or even a tunnel (made of pillows or sofa cushions) can create an interesting challenge

- ○ Create a "**Cloud Bed for Movement,**" or a "**Special Space Parachute**" like the ones in these Strength In Words blog posts

- Organize his toys in a place he can easily access

  - ○ Consider arranging them according to category (for instance, separating blocks, puzzles, toy vehicles, plush objects, books, etc.)

  - ○ This way, he knows where they can be found, and knows where they go when you "assist him" in putting things away

- *Great Resource:*

  - ○ For more information about "self-education" in movement, listen to the Strength In Words Podcast episode, "**Understanding Babies Through Movement,**" with special guest and somatic movement therapist and educator, Ania Witkowska

35 WEEKS OLD: RHYTHM AND SONG

Rhythm and Song (Communicative Development)

Books and finger plays are wonderful examples of activities that promote joint attention (theshared attention between you and your child upon an object). [17]

Many babies within this age range are interested in looking at books or listening to and watching rhymes and songs being performed for a brief period. This is related to her growing

17. Mundy, P., Newell, L. (2007). Attention, Joint Attention, and Social Cognition. Current Directions in Psychological Sciences, 16(5): 269-274.

ability to attend, her budding comprehension of words and rhythm, and her interest in relating to you.

WHAT YOU CAN DO

Give your baby both visual and auditory input by using movement and/or images as you sing or read to her.

- **Call attention to the rhythm in nursery rhymes or simple songs by alternating rhythm with song**
- **Find (or make) a book of a familiar song.**

  - ◦ Alternate singing it and reading the words to vary the experience
  - ◦ Sometimes, your baby may simply want to study the pictures. Open the book to a page that interests her and either remain silent, or point to an object and make its

"sound," label its action, etc., instead of simply reading what is on the page

○ Check out our idea to make a **"DIY Song Picture Book"** on the Strength In Words blog

36 WEEKS OLD: GIVING CHOICES AND CONTROL

Giving Choices and Control (Cognitive Development)

With added mobility comes added ability... and your baby's newfound abilities allow him to make more obvious choices about how he'd like to engage with the world.

As he learns more about the world around him, and the routines he participates in every day, he can be given opportunities to make small decisions that show he has some effect on his environment. [18]

Starting this "involvement" early can have positive effects down the line when managing more "toddler" behavior, as you are building the framework that sets clear expectations, while simultaneously allowing him to feel a sense of control within your own agenda.

18. California Department of Education, California Infant/Toddler Curriculum Framework, Sacramento, 2012, pg. 103.

WHAT YOU CAN DO

Allow him to make simple choices between no more than two visually obvious options (each of which are acceptable options to YOU!) throughout his day – in care routines, in play, and on-the-go, and indicate clearly that you've understood his preference.

- **Ensure the two options are "concretely" represented**

  - As in visually obvious, so he can look at, extend his body towards, point to one of them, or show you in some way

  - Describe the item he chose, as well, so you are intrinsically weaving in descriptive language!

- **If he does not indicate a preference, make one for him!**

  - Let him know that next time, he can pick!

  - If you can, give aloud a reason for *why* you're choosing one over the other – for example, because he enjoyed it in the past or picked it last time

- **Care routine examples:**

  - *Dressing:* hold up two clothing items he can pick from

  - *Bathing:* ask him which of two body parts you might scrub next (point to each as you label them)

  - *Eating:* hold up two drink options, flatware options, bib options, or food options

  - *Bedtime:* hold up two books he can choose from, or two cuddly animals who might want to kiss him good night

- **Play examples:**

  - Have him choose between two toys to play with next, or which one to stack / roll / manipulate in relation to another

  - Sing a song with props (stuffed animals, photos, scarves, instruments) – let him choose the prop, or once you're finished, ask which one he wants you to use next

  - *A note about forced choice during play: Too much of anything is often... too much – we want our babies to lead their own play, so try not to create too much "choice-making" in a situation that would likely be much more beneficial if it were less structured and child-led! If your baby looks to you for guidance, wants you to perform something he can't do himself, is requesting a social routine, or appears bored or unengaged with the available options, then offering a choice of some kind is a more productive thing to do in a play context!*

- **On-the-go example:**

  - *Grocery store:* hold up or point to two options of items you actually can't decide between, yourself!

- *Park/Playground:* ask him which direction he wants to explore next, pointing to the two options
- *In transit:* pick a song you know he likes, and ask him to point to, touch or hold up one of two visible items in the environment – substitute a lyric in the song with the object he's chosen

CHAPTER 4

Within this chapter, I'll suggest additional resources for you to explore on the Strength In Words website. You can find all of those resources organized by chapter here: https://www.strengthinwords.com/book-bonus

37 WEEKS OLD: IDENTITY

Identity (Social/Emotional Development)

Part of your baby's social/emotional development is learning about the fact that she has her own identity, separate from others.

Our babies (like us) learn about identity within the context of those around them. As humans, we are social, and we are born ready to take in information from others. [1] Babies learn what it is to "be human" within the context of their families and primary caregivers.

---

1. Zero to Three. (2008). Caring for infants & toddlers in groups: Developmentally appropriate practice (2nd ed.). Washington, DC: Zero to Three.

WHAT YOU CAN DO

Play games to help your baby understand with her various senses that she is her own person, separate from you, and that she comes from within a particular culture with specific values.

- **Stand or sit in front of a mirror together, and label while pointing to her body parts**

  ◦ Touch a part of her body, then show her the same part of your body – "look, here's *your* nose, and here's *my* nose!"

  ◦ Play a peek-a-boo game in the mirror by stepping away from it and asking, "where's ___?" Come close again, saying, "There she is! There's ___!"

- **Play games that involve "looking" for other people**

- ◦ Enhance her understanding that each member of the family is a separate entity – and also exists even when not in sight!

- **Validate the importance of your family's culture, language, music, and/or those that have influenced you**

  - ◦ Tell stories, read books with characters that look or do things like you, play special music, eat special foods
  - ◦ This is the beginning of her understanding of *who* she is, in relation to *where* she comes from

38 WEEKS OLD: GESTURAL COMMUNICATION

Gestural Communication (Communicative Development)

Gestures are understood to be important indicators of spoken language learning,[2] and typically start to enter your baby's repertoire of "non-verbal" communication abilities around the age of 9 months (this often happens earlier *or* later)!

There are several types of gestures, but all can be understood to convey a fairly specific meaning. This is the beginning of your baby's understanding that *language* is a collection of symbols. For instance:

Wave = Greet (hello or good-bye)

Point = Refer to something in the environment, often to make a request or call attention

Take = Take from a partner for oneself

2. L. Bloom and others, "Early Conversations and Word Learning: Contributions from Child and Adult," Child Development 67 (1996): 3154–75.

Show = hold an object up for a social purpose

Often, a gesture is accompanied by some other form of non-verbal communication – eye contact, a facial expression, a vocalization, etc. As your baby starts to use more and more concrete ways of communicating, there is often an inverse relationship with the level of frustration (both yours and his!) – he is able to tell you more about what he wants, what he thinks, and what his interests are!

WHAT YOU CAN DO

In addition to ensuring that you're modeling the above gestures in your every day life, try using a gesture to accompany certain frequently used words (actions, people, attributes, greetings, etc.)

- **Your baby is paying attention to your mouth** *and* **your extremities!**

  ◦ If you make a particular gesture to represent a word, your baby may start to associate the gesture with the word

- **You might make up your own gesture (just be consistent!) or pull from a pre-established version of** *Sign Language*

- **When singing songs, act out a gesture for an action or character**

  ◦ Finger plays, for instance are wonderful ways to encourage your baby to watch you sing and gesture!

- *Great Resource:*

  ◦ Download our free track, **"Sock Puppet Song"** (a Strength In Words original!) for a fun way to use movement, song, and gesture

39 WEEKS OLD: ENJOYING BOOKS

Enjoying Books (Communicative Development)

Within this age range, the way babies interact with books often changes quite dramatically. Your baby may go from engaging more with the physical properties of a book (shaking, crumpling, waving it) to focusing on pictures (looking at or even pointing to them). [3]

By the later stage of this age range, babies often show more traditional "enjoyment" of books, spending less time

3. Schickedanz, J.A. (1999). Much More than the ABCs: The Early Stages of Reading and Writing. Washington, D.C.: NAEYC.

manipulating them and more time engaging with the pictures and listening to the words.

Your baby may hand a book to you or point to the one she wants when given a choice, and may help you turn the page if given the chance to do so.

WHAT YOU CAN DO

Try to allow your baby to engage with books at the level she is most comfortable.

- **If your baby simply wants to turn the pages of the book or remove the books from the shelf one at a time (or all at once):**

    ○ Allow this to be the activity!

    ○ You might try to tell her one thing about the page she's looking at, or read a book aloud as she busies herself with other books.

- **Try not to feel that the "only" way to read a book is by reading the words on the page**

- It may help to find a book with *no* words, to create a book with pictures from magazines, or to find a picture book in another language.

- Instead of reading the story as it appears on the page, simply point out what you see, or make the sounds of what appears on the page. For more ideas, refer to the Strength In Words episode, **"Think Outside The Text"**

- Don't miss educator Megan Lingo's great tips for reading on the Strength In Words episode, **"Wordless Picture Books"**

- **If she is enjoying the look of a page after you've stopped reading:**

  - You might simply pause and let her look at the picture, or comment on something in the picture, before you continue

40 WEEKS OLD: SPATIAL RELATIONSHIPS

Spatial Relationships (Cognitive Development)

There is research indicating that babies as young as six months old are starting to understand certain aspects of spatial relationships between objects. [4] Infants are also beginning to detect differences between sets of small numbers of objects. [5] Both of these skills are the starting points for what eventually becomes mathematical learning.

From around 10 months, infants start to learn to form and understand spatial "categories" – we think of these as spatial

4. National Research Council. (2009). Mathematics Learning in Early Childhood: Paths Toward Excellence and Equity (Washington, DC: National Academies Press, p. 2.
5. M. M. Haith and J. B. Benson. (1998). Infant Cognition. New York: John Wiley and Sons, Inc.

or directional concepts such as *on, off, under, over, between, behind,* etc. [6]

Infants rely on familiar objects to understand words for spatial relationships, and then eventually transfer that knowledge with new or unfamiliar objects, as well. In other words, your baby uses the information he knows to learn new words and concepts! For example, your baby may be playing with his favorite ball, when it rolls out of sight and under the chair. You might say, *"Your ball is over here! It's under the chair!"* while pointing towards the ball. Your baby might follow your point and your gaze, and locate the ball under the chair, tucking away that experience with the words *ball, under* and *chair* to be added to additional experiences he has with those words (and words like them), eventually learning the meaning of more words as well as the concepts.

6. Casaola, M. (2008). The Development of Infants' Spatial Categories. Association for Psychological Science, 17(1), 21-25.

WHAT YOU CAN DO

Offer play materials that support your baby's understanding of spatial relationships, and narrate how you or your baby is relating objects to one another.

- **Offer toys that vary in size and shape, and that fit together in different ways**

  - Nesting, stacking, placing one inside another – this is a great use of those variously sized food storage containers!

- **Talk about how you or your baby is relating to the objects**

- ○ Use words for those spatial relationships and directional concepts
- ○ *"Your block is IN the cup;" "My hand is UNDER the table;" "Should we put the ball ON the tower?*

- **Sing songs or chants that involve relational and spatial concepts (and when possible, the "pair" or "opposite" word), such as:**

  - ○ On / Off
  - ○ Over / Under
  - ○ Up / Down
  - ○ Behind / In Front
  - ○ Between
  - ○ Next to *or* Beside

41 WEEKS OLD: RECOGNIZING THE FAMILIAR

Recognizing the Familiar (Communicative Development)

Around this time, babies typically begin to recognize words for common items – things with which they are in contact on a regular basis, such as "cup," "book," or "shoe." *(Obviously, specific vocabulary can vary and is unique to each family and situation!)*

You may also notice that your baby has started to recognize familiar "social routines" – games which are played whose rules he can anticipate, or caregiving routines such as diapering or bathing.

WHAT YOU CAN DO

Help your baby learn to anticipate the "next step" by engaging in routines or rituals throughout the day, and talk about what you're doing.

- **Narrate to him what the** *first,* *next,* **and** *last* **step is as you go through these steps during familiar routines.**

  ◦ On the changing pad, as you get ready for bath or bedtime, or as he wakes up in the morning

- **Play games like peek-a-boo and sing/chant nursery rhymes (adding hand movements when you can)**

  ◦ Your baby may really start to enjoy those that have a special ending or type of movement (he gets tickled or lifted up, he gets to see your face appear in a wide grin, etc.)

42 WEEKS OLD: PROCESSES

Processes (Social/Emotional Development)

As your baby becomes more mobile, as routines become predictable, and as her understanding of words increases (especially those used within familiar routines!), she can predict what will happen and participate more fully in familiar "events" such as diapering, feeding, dressing washing, & greeting.

Because these routines occur throughout the day, every day, they offer the opportunity for important learning. When your baby is able to participate, she develops an understanding about her own body, learns how to read you and your expectations, and becomes a part of the process.

As your baby learns more about her body (how to move it, how to satiate hunger and other needs) she will begin to move as she sees fit – which may or may not be in line with your needs!

Gund Baby Animated Flappy The Elephant Plush Toy

amazon Gift Receipt

Send a Thank You Note

You can learn more about your gift or start a return here too.

Scan using the Amazon app or visit
http://a.co/c4YBv8c

A gift for you

Hi Addison, Enjoy your gift! From
Rheggy

WHAT YOU CAN DO

Give her opportunities to participate in any way she can. Give words for what you are doing, and try to make the experience more enjoyable.

- **Sing a familiar tune with word about the "process" of what you're doing**

  - Sometimes, simply shifting from speaking to singing will be enough to focus your baby's attention and calm her body

- **Provide opportunities within routines for your baby to "participate" at her level**

  - *Greeting (hello, good-bye):* Pause after you say hello or good-bye to allow your baby time to respond, as you would for anyone else in the conversation

    - Then give language for the way you see her participating (i.e., "*I saw you look back at me! Yes, hello!*" or, "*Oh, thank you for that smile,*" "*What a lovely wave!*")

    - If you feel your baby does not respond in any way, try not to manipulate her body – and understand that there may have been more forces at work than you were aware (she may have needed more time to process, she may have been focused on learning something else, etc.)

  - *Diapering and Dressing/Undressing:* Offer a sock, sleeve, trouser leg, etc. in a way that *suggests* you are going to put it on her body

    - Pause near the body part, for instance

    - Tell her, "it's time to put your sock on," make a funny

sound as you get ready to do it, or change your pace (doing things exaggeratedly quickly or slowly)

- *Feeding*: Offer soft finger foods that she can pick up herself, and/or small amounts of water or milk in an open cup with handles so she can feed herself. Offer her own utensil to hold (or to drop, as the case may be!)

- *Washing:* Give her a washcloth to hold, or a towel to dry herself

  - Ask her what she wants you to wash next (offering two choices by pointing to and naming them)

  - Even if she doesn't point at or look at her own body to tell you, you are involving her in the process (and she's hearing the vocabulary!)

- **Respond to her if she becomes frustrated**

  - Research shows that infants who are frustrated or upset benefit greatly from a caregiver who helps them manage their distress or frustration (rather than ignore it or tell her simply that "she'll be fine") [7]

  - Explain and *show* what you expect from her, let her know what you can do to help her, and shift gears to a new activity or position as soon as you are able

  - It may be that in this moment, she is simply unable to focus or participate!

43 WEEKS OLD: CAUSE AND EFFECT

Cause and Effect (Cognitive Development)

7. K. L. Rosenblum, C. J. Dayton, & M. Muzik. (2009). Infant Social and Emotional Development: Emerging Competence in a Relational Context. Handbook of Infant Mental Health (3rd ed). New York, NY: Guilford Publishers.

As your baby explores his world more and more, you will likely catch him "practicing" skills over and over again. [8] This allows him to experiment with the notion that his body and his actions have an effect on the world: a cause and an effect.

He may be solidifying his understanding of cause and effect at any time of day, and within any type of activity! It may be through a repeated action during "play" time (i.e., knocking down or throwing blocks), physical activity (i.e., crawling or walking up and down a stair), meal time (i.e., dropping his spoon, plate, cup, food, etc.), or other daily routine – or all of the above!

Though it may, at times, feel like your baby is "testing" *you*, the intention is to test theories about the *world*. This is the way he learns!

8. California Department of Education, California Infant/Toddler Curriculum Framework, Sacramento, 2012, pg. 105-106.

WHAT YOU CAN DO

By shifting your perspective and remembering that he is not trying to be naughty (and instead is trying to conduct scientific experiments), work with him to allow him to explore in a safe and productive way. This will likely require you to think flexibly and find a solution that is acceptable to both of you!

- **Ensure safety**

  ◦ If your baby has chosen a particularly busy stair on which to explore gravity, try to find a way to make it safe

  ◦ Help guide him to the side where there is less traffic, and show him how to move his body to place his legs down first, rather than his head

- **Offer an alternative**

  ◦ If your baby is repeatedly knocking down the tower you've built, make it into a game and see how many blocks you can build before he gets to them!

  ◦ If he is throwing blocks, help him to throw or place them in a bowl or box

- **Acknowledge what he is communicating through his actions**

  ◦ If your baby is dropping or clearing his eating area, tell him what his actions *tell you*

  ◦ "It looks like you're all done with the sweet potato! None of it has gone in your mouth – it's all going on the floor!"

- **Make the time, whenever possible**

  ◦ If your baby is working on a particular skill, it will likely translate into new abilities and shifts in his development – in ways that you could not have foreseen!

○ When we give our babies time to practice what interests them, we are allowing them to guide their learning needs – a completely developmentally appropriate framework for learning in these early years

44 WEEKS OLD: SYMBOLS AND SOUNDS

Symbols and Sounds (Communicative Development)

The acquisition of words to make language is essentially a set of symbols: each symbol or set of sounds = a word that represents a thing / idea / person

Calling attention to certain representations of objects, people or ideas in the environment can highlight this concept for your baby

WHAT YOU CAN DO

In your home and community, highlight symbols: talk about iconography you see by pointing to the "green man" for walking across the street, the "woman" on the door to the toilet," the "stop sign" to stop

- **When in or out, highlight letters (by pointing them out and making their letter sounds)**

  ◦ Alphabet blocks: when stacking (or destroying!), simply say the letter or letter sound you see

  ◦ Alphabet books: make (or buy) a book with an image that starts with each letter

    ▪ To make, you might use images from magazines/ internet search of familiar objects / places / actions /

feelings by placing images in sheet protectors or on card stock

- **When in your home, highlight environmental sounds (drip-drop, whooosh or boom!), social sounds (uh oh! Shh... wow!), animal sounds (moo, bah, meow)**

  ○ *Book reading:* instead of reading the words on the page (and even instead of naming *what* you see), make the *sounds* of what you see: point to the sink and say, "shhhhhhh" or "drip drop," or point to a car and say, "vroooom!"

  ○ *House Hunt:*

    ▪ For babies not yet on the move, walk into different rooms and either point to objects and make "their sound," or make a sound about what you might do with it or a preposition you use with it (point to or sit on the bed and say anything from "snore!" or "ahhhh" or "in," "down" or "sleeeep!")

    ▪ For babies who are mobile, follow their lead! Anything they focus on, explore, experiment with – make that noise!

45 WEEKS OLD: CORE STRENGTHENING IN PLAY

Core Strengthening in Play (Motor Development)

As adults, we are told that some of the best exercises are those that "strengthen our core." The core muscles are those within the tummy, back and pelvis.

From infancy, we use these muscles, the development of which allows us to balance, coordinate movement, sit up straight, etc.

Many movements that babies do everyday are naturally core-strengthening, but creating opportunities for those who are beginning to sit, crawl, and walk can help us facilitate and encourage these activities.

WHAT YOU CAN DO

Encourage activities that involve rolling, lifting/picking up objects, pushing or pulling

- **Roll:** Rolling over and rolling around can be great fun on surfaces that make a sound or that are textured in some way (i.e., crinkled or tissue paper, bubble wrap, contact paper)
- **Lift:** Place objects that might be interesting on either side of

your baby so she can pick up objects that are interesting by reaching in different ways

- Encourage her to move an object from one side of her body into a container on her other side (this facilitates "crossing the midline," or moving something from one side of the body to the other side) – this helps build pathways in the brain, and requires both sides of the brain to work together!

- **Push (pre-crawlers)**: Place a ball in front of your baby, and push it toward her hand. Give her opportunities to push or swat at it. On her belly, help her use her feet to push against you (propelling forward) to grab a toy just out of reach

- **Push (crawlers):** Model to her how she can move a lighter-weight object across the floor (such as a laundry basket, a cardboard box, a shopping bag) and do it with her – taking turns might make it more fun!

- **Push (weight-bearing on feet or walkers)**: Encourage her to push a lighter chair or taller box (so her arms can reach out and she doesn't have to do much bending) across the room while standing up

- **Pull**: Pull scarves or napkins out of a box with a hole in it (such as a tissue box or empty wipe container), pull a blanket out of a basket, pull a toy on a string, etc.)

- *Great Resource:*

  - For additional activities involving **"Heavy Work,"** check out our DIY blog post from Strength In Words!

46 WEEKS OLD: MOOD SENSITIVITY

Mood Sensitivity (Social/Emotional Development)

Even in the first year of life, babies are incredibly sensitive to emotion. Research suggests that already by a few months of age, infants are able to recognize the difference between happy and sad expressions, and differentially process emotional tones in voices they hear. [9]

Recent findings also suggest that infants exposed to more conflict show higher stress levels (measured by their brain activity to angry tones of voice) – and regular exposure to conflict (*including exposure while they are asleep!*) can deeply affect the way their brains process emotion and anxiety, which in turn affects their own ability to learn to regulate emotions. [10]

You may have seen your baby start to cry simply when she hears another baby cry! This imitation is not simply for the sake of imitating others, but because infants look to others for cues about emotional signals, and are affected by other peoples' emotions. [11]

9. Soken, N. H. and Pick, A. D. (1999), Infants' Perception of Dynamic Affective Expressions: Do Infants Distinguish Specific Expressions?. Child Development, 70: 1275–1282.
10. Graham, A.M., Fisher, P.A., Pfeifer, J.H. (2013). What sleeping babies hear: a functional MRI study of inter parental conflict and infants' emotion processing. Psychological Science 24(5), 782-789.
11. T. Striano and P. Rochat. (2000). Emergence of Selective Social Referencing in Infancy. Infancy 1(2), 253–64.

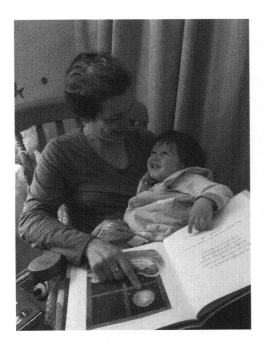

WHAT YOU CAN DO

Try to pay attention to your emotional reactions to things, and give words for how you (or others around you) are feeling.

- **Be aware of how often you use an angry voice in front of your baby**

  - When you do argue in front of her, make an attempt to resolve the issue in front of her, as well!

- **Label emotions**

  - Of people in your environment (at the park, in the bus, in a book, in your home), especially when strong emotions are witnessed

- **Explain how actions make people feel**

- ○ When looking at pictures of other people, make predictions about why they might feel a certain way

- **In general, when speaking to your baby, try to match your tone with your intent**

  - ○ Sarcasm is lost on your infant (or toddler!)

  - ○ Your baby is learning from you about how to display and regulate her emotional reactions to things, so the clearer you can be about yours, the more information you give her to use

47 WEEKS OLD: SUPPORTED FREE PLAY

Supported Free Play (Motor Development)

Your baby can gain many developmentally appropriate learning opportunities from "free play," or the freedom to choose what *he* wants to do.

Giving babies opportunities to learn in a non-structured setting is more likely to develop their attention span and motor skills when provided with opportunities to choose *with what* and *where* to play. [12] [13]

Babies in this age range, especially, tend to do a lot of repeating of the same activity – practicing the same movement (or set of movements) to figure out how things work, and strengthening the connections they make in their brains.

12. Pikler, E. (1971). Learning of motor skills on the basis of self-induced movements. In Exceptional Infant, vol. 2, ed. J. Hellmuth, 54–89. New York: Bruner/Mazel.
13. Bergen, D., Reid, R., and Torelli, L. (2009). Educating and Caring for Very Young Children: The Infant/Toddler Curriculum (2nd ed.). New York, NY: Teachers College Press.

WHAT YOU CAN DO

Place interesting objects near your baby to encourage him to reach out, move around, touch and manipulate. Allow him access to familiar places and objects to give him the opportunity to practice and solidify the skills on which he is working

- **Vary the objects you offer and the "plane" on which you offer them (on the ground, in a box, on top of a table, etc.)**

  - This, of course, depends on his level of mobility
  - Allow him to practice using different muscles and problem-solve how to get certain places
  - Make sure you place objects just far enough that he can

challenge himself, but not far enough that it becomes too frustrating

- **Try to vary the environment**

  - Provide time both in and out of doors, explore natural elements (i.e., grass, sand, plants, water) as well as toys and common household or natural materials
  - This allows your baby to explore and experience a good mixture of textural and sensory information

- **Instead of guiding your baby to perform a specific task with an object:**

  - Talk about what she *is* doing, what she might be looking at
  - Explain how the object work or what it does
  - Comment on similarities or differences between what she's studying and other things around her
  - Encourage her to continue what she's doing (assuming she's safe!)

- **You can model for her the way *you* might interact with the object, but her learning will be far more meaningful if she discovers new ways to engage with the world on her own.**

  - For an explanation of the ways young children learn through experience, listen to the Strength In Words podcast episode, **"Experiential Learning"**
  - Check out our blog post on how to make a **"Book Reading and Prop Play Basket"** for a wonderful idea to integrate experience with music/rhythm & early literacy!

48 WEEKS OLD: ATTENTION MAINTENANCE

Attention Maintenance (Cognitive Development)

Babies in this age range are likely only to spend a few minutes with any single toy or activity before turning to something new. By 12 months, a particularly interesting or favorite activity *may occasionally* hold his attention for up to 10 minutes or so. This is perfectly appropriate for children of this age, and as an infant becomes more mobile, he finds more ways to experience and learn about the things and people in his environment. He may move quickly from one thing to the next, making his own connections and taking in information.

Although some parents find that their children of this age are calm and "attentive" to a screen (television, tablet, mobile device) for longer periods, research shows that this is not a way to build a child's attention maintenance ability (as in, it will not "carry over" to other activities). The reason behind this is essentially that "screen time" such as this is a passive activity – simply *watching* a two-dimensional object is not an active or socially interactive activity.

What *does* help to extend attention, developmental researchers have found, is open-ended play. Allowing infants and toddlers the opportunity to explore different aspects of their environment in new ways without a specific "end-game" or agenda (i.e., without expecting them to perform a task) is the key to allowing your baby to learn and to stay engaged for longer periods of time. [14]

This requires caregivers to be more active observers and providers of loose guidance, rather than "organizers" or even

14. Bergen, D., Reid, R., and Torelli, L. (2009). Educating and Caring for Very Young Children: The Infant/Toddler Curriculum (2nd ed.). New York, NY: Teachers College Press.

"teachers," and shifts the focus to the *means* of play rather than the *end-goal*, in the moment that we are engaging with our child. Most importantly, it requires us to be flexible!

WHAT YOU CAN DO

Set up items in a play area in new ways, give access to new or different items or in different combinations, model different ways to interact with familiar objects.

- **Set up a "tableau" in an area your baby normally plays**

  ◦ Arrange her toys in new or silly ways to call attention to objects she hasn't seen in relation to each other

- **Play with materials that you have partially hidden**

  ◦ She might have to remove them from a container

- **Accessing new materials allows her to explore the ways things are similar and different to those she already knows**

  ◦ Take a "nature walk" together, and either explore natural

materials in the outdoors, or bring them back inside and explore them in relation to household objects (i.e., leaves, flower petals, rocks, twigs, acorns, pine cones, etc.)

◦ Play "peek-a-boo" with new or different materials, including natural materials you find outside

• *Great Resource:*

◦ Check out our Strength In Words podcast episode, **"3 Ways To Use Routines In Play"** with speech-language pathologist, Lia Kurtin.

49 WEEKS OLD: PLAYING WITH PICTURES

Playing With Pictures (Communication Development)

As your baby starts to use more gestures (i.e., pointing, waving, nodding/shaking his head, clapping, etc.) and grows to engage with books in a more "traditional" sense (at times, being able to sit for a few minutes and focus with you on the pictures), you will likely find yourself asking him questions about the pictures he sees.

It is easy to find yourself caught in a "drill and practice" scenario, asking him, "where's this, where's that?" again and again. There is nothing wrong with asking this particular question, or with using flashcards with your baby, but remember that showing your baby an image and expecting him to respond in a "correct" way, "point to the ___," "where's the ___" is simply a labeling activity: you're asking him to engage in a VERY limited part of *all the reasons and ways we communicate!*

Instead of using picture books or images in magazines to simply ask your child to label objects or people, consider shifting the focus of the entire activity to make it more communicative – so you are *both* part of the activity. Don't hesitate to point out objects that *you* notice, as well, and try to treat it like any other conversation, where you both have something to say! This is more likely to capture your child's attention for a longer period of time, as well, as it is more natural engagement and interaction (vs. a testing scenario).

WHAT YOU CAN DO

Not only can you find images within a picture to label, you can also relate them to personal experiences your baby has had with people, places or objects.

- **Consider all the things you could say about a picture, by asking yourself to answer questions that start with:**

    ◦ Who / What / When / Where AND Why

- For instance, who is in the picture? "I see a boy with his friend... Let's think of who some of your friends are!"

- **Make the sounds of the things you see**

  - Rushing water in a waterfall, a dog barking, a house with a front door that goes, "knock, knock!," a person smiling who says, "smile!" or "I'm so happy!"

- **Sing a song about all the people or things you see**

  - Use a familiar tune, such as "Wheels on the Bus" – "the dog in the park says, 'ruff, ruff, ruff!'"

- **If you do ask your baby to label, make it into a game!**

  - "Can *you* find the ___?" Ask him once, and then pause! Be aware of how many times you're asking the same question... your baby needs time to process and search!

- **Be mindful of what your *baby* finds interesting about the picture.**

  - Sit back and just look at the picture together
  - You may find that your baby starts to point to something he's interested in, or notices something that you never did!
  - Follow his gaze and look at what he is focusing on – and then talk about *that*

50 WEEKS OLD: WAS IT A WORD?

Was It A Word? (Communicative Development)

In the days, weeks or even months preceding that "first word," we often hear *proto-words* (pre words). There is no specific content within them, but they can be repeated again and again, with the same sounds (they are phonetically consistent), and they seem purposeful – as if your baby is *really* saying something to you!

Sometimes these *proto-words* are used within the same context (i.e., "mummmmm" when she reaches for the breast to nurse). It is always a good idea to assume intentionality, and use your baby's non-verbal cues (such as gestures, eye gaze, facial expression, vocalization, etc.) to help make an educated guess about what she wants or is trying to express).

A *true*, "first word" has a more specific definition, very rarely appears before around 11 – 12 months, and can easily emerge several months later! It can be defined by *all of* the following: [15]

- Consistency: you hear it over and over again, often in the same context

- Use in appropriate context: you hear it in the same context across different situations, often using non-verbal cues (i.e., your baby says *"nana"* while *pointing* to and *looking at* the banana

- Recognizable speech sounds: the word may not be pronounced correctly, but the "essence" is there – i.e., your baby says *"wawa"* for "water"

- Spontaneous utterance: your baby utters the word spontaneously, as in, on her own and not in imitation

The earliest words to appear are often nouns (words that represent familiar people, food, play materials, body parts, animals, clothes, places, etc.) Other common first words might include greetings, or the word, "no!" In this age range, much of what babies understand is *in context*. Therefore, the words

15. McLaughlin, S. (2006). Introduction to Language Development (2nd ed.). Clifton, NY: Thomson Delmar Learning.

a baby first says are often contextually based in familiar environments and with familiar partners, and are based on her preferences. In other words, if your child has never seen a hot dog, chances are, that won't be her first word!

WHAT YOU CAN DO

First and foremost, of course, TALK to your baby! Talk about what you are doing, where you're going, what she's doing, what's coming next, etc.

- **During caregiving routines**

  - Encourage her to use gestures and vocalizations
  - Ask her questions and pause expectantly for her answer

- **Honor gestures as specific communication**

  - Representational (i.e. waving "hi/bye," shaking head "no") and referential (i.e., pointing at something specific) gestures are very clear attempts at communication
  - Narrate the words to which your baby is referring

- **Model one step above**

  - If your baby points to a car, you might point as well, and say, "yes, a car!," modeling both the gesture *and* the word

  - Your baby will imitate when she is ready, but you can make the next step in her development very clear!

- **If your baby is beginning to use words (or signs)**

  - Acknowledge that you heard what was said, and model it back with the "adult" pronunciation

  - If your baby is requesting a person or object, either supply it right away, or offer an alternative: "water! You want some water. Here it is." or "I hear you call for 'Mama,' but she's at work right now! Let's look at some pictures of her."

  - Repeat the word back, and offer *one more* bit of information: "Yes, a car. It's a *blue car*"

- *Great Resource:*

  - Don't miss the Strength In Words podcast episode, "**5 Strategies to Promote Communication in Your Young Child,**" with speech-language pathologist Carrie Clark

51 WEEKS OLD: ENVIRONMENTAL EXPLORATION

Environmental Exploration (Motor Development)

When young children are able to choose what and how to play with objects around them, they are more likely to explore their environment. [16]

16. Bergen, D., Reid, R., and Torelli, L. (2009). Educating and Caring for Very Young Children: The Infant/Toddler Curriculum (2nd ed.). New York, NY: Teachers College Press.

In a safe environment with interesting options, they are able to reach, move and explore! This allows them to experience the world from both a movement and sensory perspective, integrating information and discerning ways certain experiences are similar or dissimilar to other experiences they've had.

WHAT YOU CAN DO

Provide your little one with safe play spaces (on the floor, in the community) to explore and investigate his environment, and so he can roll, crawl, walk, and stretch!

- Limit the use of equipment that restricts your child's movement
- Introduce opportunities to experience various textures (e.g., wet, dry, smooth, rough, muddy) so your baby can experiment

- ○ Messy play experiences *can* be more contained for the more resistant adult, as well! Don't miss the Strength In Words podcast episode, **"What's So Great About Messy Play?"** for additional discussion, examples, and suggestions

52 WEEKS OLD: FUNCTIONAL OBJECT EXPLORATION

Functional Object Exploration (Cognitive Development)

Your little one enjoys exploring objects in different ways to understand their properties. As she observes and imitates you, she is starting to associate familiar objects with their function – e.g., a spoon is something you put in your mouth when eating, a brush is something you put in your hair.

This is the start of an era when you'll likely *start* to see a slow emergence of "symbolic play" as well. Symbolic play is essentially the use of an object as "representative" of another object. [17] For example, the child plays with a block to represent an ice cube in a pitcher, a car "vrooming" across the floor, or a brush that combs a doll's hair. Symbolic play and "pretend play" often go hand in hand.

---

17. Best Start Expert Panel on Early Learning. (2007). Early Learning for Every Child Today: A Framework for Ontario Early Childhood Settings. Ontario: pg 16.

WHAT YOU CAN DO

Talk about what you're doing, why you're doing those things, and what comes next. Your little one is watching and listening, and often imitating your actions. She's also experimenting with objects in her own way – it might not always appear that she's doing things intentionally, but she's always learning!

- **When your baby shakes or bangs an object, she is experimenting with concepts such as weight, texture, etc.**

  - Give words for the objects, their properties and her actions

- **Model various ways to use household objects and play materials, and try to give your baby access to real objects or "child sized" versions (e.g., pots and wooden spoons for stirring)**

- Engage in both "real" interactions and pretend play with your child. For instance, if you're stirring a pot on the stove and lean over to smell or taste it, you can say, "mmmm!" – do the same thing down on the floor with her in a play routine, using her pot and spoon

- Follow your child's lead! Model these interactions, but if she wants to bang on the pot instead, you might bang too, and turn it into a rhythm activity!

What's Next

WHERE TO GO FROM HERE?

The ideas in this book are simple for a reason: you already have everything it takes to support your baby. Sometimes it simply takes a bit of hand-holding and a friendly fist bump from another mama who's been through the trenches (and who knows that there's no right or wrong way to be a parent). Regardless of how many – or how few – of the modules you've gone through, I sincerely hope the information within this book has provided you with a good place to start when it comes to interacting with and learning about your baby.

If you enjoyed *Understanding Your Baby,* I hope you'll take a moment to review it on Amazon. This will help other new parents and caregivers find resources that help them. In fact, I hope you'll share this book with your friends or family who are expecting a new baby – after all, what better gift could you give a new or expecting parent than the gift of knowledge?

The learning doesn't stop here. We weren't meant to parent in isolation! Readers of *Understanding Your Baby* and followers of Strength In Words report **greater satisfaction and more embracive results** within the context of our community and content hub, the Strength In Words Community LAB. The

Community LAB is a virtual parent support and parent education platform. It is a membership community for families with infants and toddlers of all developmental levels.

Inside, you'll find:

- Regular live events (including Q&A workshops with professionals, virtual developmental music classes, parent support groups and "co-parenting" workshops)

- An ever-growing, well-organized resource library (of past events, information, discussion, and ideas put forth by professionals and community members)

- The opportunity to interact *with other families* with the developmental curriculum covered in this book

- A social network to lift each other up – giving you access to a place where you can have adult conversations about your babbling baby, ask honest questions, and share experiences and ideas – never "one-size-fits-all" parenting advice.

We are a generous, caring community that values good citizenship, diversity in perspective, and respectful interactions.

If this sounds like a place you'd like to experience, I invite you to join us for a free trial at community.strengthinwords.com.
Strength In Words is the place for parents and caregivers to help their infants and toddlers learn and develop through high-quality, evidence-based resources and through connections to other parents and professionals. We are changing the ways parents access developmental resources and parental support by providing virtual access to a community of support, live interactive events, and opportunities to engage in simple, positive family interactions. We see parenthood as the great equalizer.

Regardless of cultural, linguistic or socio-economic background, all parents face the enormous responsibility of raising humans. Strength In Words focuses on empowering the family through knowledge and connection, nurturing parents so they can nurture their children. We help parents and caregivers recognize the value of everyday interactions to support their baby's development, and teach them to utilize everyday objects to support all aspects of early development. Healthy, happy families result in healthy, strong societies.

I hope you'll visit us online at Strength In Words, subscribe to the podcast, and enjoy the bonus materials that come along with your purchase of this book! If you've managed to somehow get through the whole book without grabbing these, don't forget to do that here: https://www.strengthinwords.com/book-bonus

www.strengthinwords.com

Ayelet Marinovich, M.A. CCC-SLP

Made in the USA
San Bernardino, CA
28 April 2018